teach yourself

ayurveda

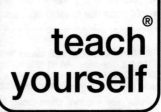

teach yourself

ayurveda
sarah lie

For over 60 years, more than 50 million people have learnt over 750 subjects the **teach yourself** way, with impressive results.

be where you want to be
with **teach yourself**

For UK order enquiries: please contact Bookpoint Ltd, 130 Milton Park, Abingdon, Oxon, OX14 4SB. Telephone: +44 (0) 1235 827720. Fax: +44 (0) 1235 400454. Lines are open 09.00–17.00, Monday to Saturday, with a 24-hour message answering service. Details about our titles and how to order are available at www.teachyourself.co.uk

For USA order enquiries: please contact McGraw-Hill Customer Services, PO Box 545, Blacklick, OH 43004-0545, USA. Telephone: 1-800-722-4726. Fax: 1-614-755-5645.

For Canada order enquiries: please contact McGraw-Hill Ryerson Ltd, 300 Water St, Whitby, Ontario, L1N 9B6, Canada. Telephone: 905 430 5000. Fax: 905 430 5020.

Long renowned as the authoritative source for self-guided learning – with more than 50 million copies sold worldwide – the **teach yourself** series includes over 500 titles in the fields of languages, crafts, hobbies, business, computing and education.

British Library Cataloguing in Publication Data: a catalogue record for this title is available from the British Library.

Library of Congress Catalog Card Number: on file.

First published in UK 2007 by Hodder Education, 338 Euston Road, London, NW1 3BH.

First published in US 2007by The McGraw-Hill Companies, Inc.

The **teach yourself** name is a registered trade mark of Hodder Headline.

Typeset by Transet Limited, Coventry, England.
Printed in Great Britain for Hodder Education, a division of Hodder Headline, 338 Euston Road, London, NW1 3BH, by Cox & Wyman Ltd, Reading, Berkshire.

The publisher has used its best endeavours to ensure that the URLs for external websites referred to in this book are correct and active at the time of going to press. However, the publisher and the author have no responsibility for the websites and can make no guarantee that a site will remain live or that the content will remain relevant, decent or appropriate.

Hodder Headline's policy is to use papers that are natural, renewable and recyclable products and made from wood grown in sustainable forests. The logging and manufacturing processes are expected to conform to the environmental regulations of the country of origin.

Impression number   10 9 8 7 6 5 4 3 2 1
Year   2010 2009 2008 2007

contents

introduction		ix
part one	the essence of ayurveda	1
01	about ayurveda and why we need it today	3
	what is ayurveda?	4
	the definition of health	4
	the origins of ayurveda	5
	the relevance of ayurveda today	6
	simple truths to keep in mind	7
02	the core philosophy	9
	a 'back-to-basics' approach	10
	the five elements (panchamahabhutas)	10
	the three doshas (vata, pitta, kapha)	12
	qualities of the mind	16
	the concept of prakriti (unique mind–body type)	17
	the role of the gunas (20 qualities)	18
	summary	20
03	the causes of disease and how to avoid them	21
	how to achieve good health	22
	the law of similarity and dissimilarity	22
	how time influences our health	23
	the power of the mind	25
	abusing our senses	28
	the importance of good digestion	29

	protecting our immunity	31
	summary	32
04	**traditional methods of healing**	**33**
	ayurveda's approach to treatment and prevention	34
	three steps for healing disease	34
	two methods of treatment – pacify or purge	35
	the five methods of internal cleansing	39
	fasting as an alternative to panchakarma	40
	revitalizing your mind and body	45
part two	**putting ayurveda into practice**	**49**
05	**getting started**	**51**
	building your ayurvedic way of life	52
	identifying your mind–body type	52
	your dosha-finder questionnaire	54
	more about your constitutional type	58
	seven-day diet to cleanse and fortify your digestion	65
	a daily dose of herbal rejuvenation	67
	mental rasayanas	68
06	**how, when and what to eat**	**70**
	food as a form of medicine	71
	the power of taste	72
	eating to suit your mind–body type	93
	eating to suit the time of day, year and life	102
	healthy eating habits	103
	the importance of food combining	106
	specific features of key food items	107
	summary	111
07	**daily and seasonal routines**	**112**
	the art of healthy living	113
	a healthy daily routine	113
	morning routine	114
	lunchtime routine	138

	evening routine	139
	seasonal guidelines	140
08	**breathing and meditation**	**146**
	the origins of pranayama and meditation	147
	the secrets of controlled breathing	148
	some simple meditation practices	152
	using mantras to meditate	154
09	**healing herbs, spices and formulations**	**157**
	natural medicines for everyday complaints	158
	healing herbs from your kitchen cupboard	159
	common herbal remedies	168
	authentic ayurvedic formulations	175
10	**self-healing secrets for common complaints**	**178**
	holistic methods of healing	179
	the next step	209
part three	**taking it further**	**211**
appendix 1	**food guidelines for the basic mind–body types**	**213**
appendix 2	**useful contacts**	**228**
appendix 3	**further reading**	**233**
appendix 4	**glossary of sanskrit terms**	**234**
index		**239**

dedication

Teach yourself Ayurveda is dedicated to all those people who are seeking to build a healthier way of life for themselves and their loved ones that is in harmony with nature.

This book would not have been possible without the help of some very generous and knowledgeable people. Firstly I wish to thank Ayurvedic practitioners, Sascha and Rebecca Kriese, for the guidance and input they have so selflessly contributed throughout the research and compilation of this book. Also my friend and fellow writer, Patrick Barclay, for his encouragement and words of wisdom on the art of book writing and last – but most certainly not least – a special word of thanks to my yoga teacher, Jilly Vainer, from whom I have learnt so much about the benefits and gifts of yoga over the past few years and whose advice on the yoga practices included in this book has been invaluable.

introduction

In today's stressful and time-pressured world good health is a vital commodity. Without a healthy mind and body we struggle to cope with the pressures of day-to-day living, the demands of our jobs, relationships, families, friends and personal needs. The impact of our multi-media, celebrity-driven culture means we also worry increasingly about the ageing process and how to stay youthful.

This helps to explain the growing demand for Ayurveda, a complete system of medicine which uses a potent blend of diet, natural remedies, lifestyle advice, rejuvenation and detoxification processes, hands-on therapies such as massage, as well as meditation and the principles of 'wise' living, according to yogic philosophy, to preserve physical and psychological health, heal disease if it does occur and – above all – promote a long and healthy life.

As the world's oldest medical system, much has been written about Ayurveda – and a mountain of knowledge accumulated – since it originated in India more than 5,000 years ago. Put simply, it is the art of healthy living.

Right now, there is a real need for us to build the wisdom of Ayurveda into our daily lives. Health experts tell us that as much as 80 per cent of our health problems today are due to inadequate diet, exercise and the stresses of modern life. This can be seen in the rapid growth of lifestyle-related diseases such as diabetes and obesity and the prevalence of anxiety, depression and other mental health problems.

While Ayurveda is a complex and extensive system of medicine it also contains a wealth of 'simple truths' that we can easily build into our everyday routines to help boost our mental and physical health. Its vast pharmacopoeia of healing herbs, spices and minerals provides us with a host of natural ways to treat everyday complaints and more serious diseases safely and effectively.

The Ayurvedic system provides invaluable healthcare information and insights as well as powerful therapeutic tools and remedies. For instance, it explains:

- the inherent causes of disease and how to avoid them
- how to determine your own unique mind and body type and maintain this natural balance to preserve good health
- which diseases you are particularly susceptible to and how to avoid them
- the importance of good digestion and how to achieve it
- what forms of exercise and environment are best suited to your particular mind and body type
- daily and seasonal regimens to preserve health and prevent disease
- effective ways to build immunity and minimize the impact of age
- when and how to detoxify and rejuvenate your mind and body
- potent and safe natural remedies for common complaints including insomnia, depression, fertility problems, the menopause, constipation and weight loss
- how judicious living, meditation and breathing exercises can be used to manage stress and improve mental health
- the use of sensory therapies such as sound, colour and aromatherapy.

I first discovered Ayurveda when I read a contemporary book on its principles and effects in 2000. I was so inspired by the practical insights this unique system of medicine offers into how to achieve a balanced, happy and healthy life, that I enrolled on the first accredited degree course to be established outside India. I qualified as an Ayurvedic practitioner in 2004, after working in three Ayurvedic hospitals in India. What I have seen and learned has convinced me that this ancient science has much to teach us about how to keep our minds and bodies well and our immunity strong in the high-pressure modern world.

Building Ayurveda into your life brings huge rewards, but it does take time and effort. That's because it is a complete way of life that looks at all the external and internal influences on our minds and bodies and how to balance them, naturally, in line with our own unique constitutional type. This book aims to equip you with the basic knowledge and tools needed to build Ayurvedic dietary, lifestyle and therapeutic practices into your everyday life, easily and effectively. To deliver this, it focuses on the authentic Ayurvedic remedies and therapies that are generally available today. While many minor ailments can be safely and effectively managed with some simple home remedies, it is important for you to use your awareness and consult a qualified Ayurvedic practitioner or doctor if you think your condition is more serious.

Ayurveda literally translates as 'the science of life'. It is the art of living in harmony with nature, to preserve health and heal disease by balancing our innate constitutional type via entirely natural means. It is based on the central principle that every one of us has a totally unique mental and physical constitution; a concept that mirrors the modern medical view that each of us has a unique genetic blueprint of DNA. To stay healthy, this constitutional balance must be maintained. That sounds pretty simple – and it is – but we need to take into account the fact that our internal body clock and external environment are constantly changing, and take steps to adjust our diet, lifestyle and behaviour accordingly, for health to be preserved.

Consider, for example, the impact time has on our minds and bodies via the ageing process; how changes in the weather and seasons trigger coughs, colds and skin problems. Consider how events at work and home can make us feel happy, anxious, tired or depressed. Unless we know how to adjust our diets, lifestyle and behaviour to counteract these influences and maintain our body's natural balance, our immunity can become impaired, allowing disease to take hold.

The ultimate goal of Ayurveda is to promote long life by optimizing our body's natural defences (immunity) and so minimizing the impact of time. In Ayurveda this is called 'rasayana' or rejuvenation therapy.

The aim of this book is to simplify the wealth of knowledge and experience contained in the authoritative Ayurvedic texts, into a practical, easy-to-use guide for everyday healthy living. It will take some effort on your part, but applying the wisdom of Ayurveda to your everyday life really can lead to greater happiness, health and longevity for you and your family.

part one

the essence of Ayurveda

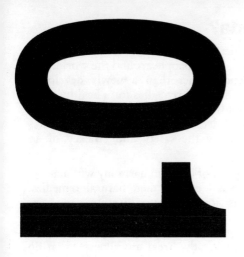

01

about Ayurveda and why we need it today

In this chapter you will learn:
- what Ayurveda is
- its definition of health
- why this system of holistic healthcare is so relevant today
- the basic principles for healthy living
- some simple truths about putting Ayurveda into practice.

What is Ayurveda?

Ayurveda is the world's oldest holistic healthcare system and the medicine of choice for millions of people around the world. It is a complete medical science rather than a newly developed alternative therapy. Its theories and remedies for a healthy mind and body have endured for more than 5,000 years, during which time a wealth of knowledge and practical experience has been accumulated, confirming the safety and efficacy of an Ayurvedic way of life.

Essentially, Ayurveda is the art of living in harmony with nature. It teaches us how to use a blend of diet, natural remedies, lifestyle practices, rejuvenation and detoxification processes, hands-on therapies such as massage, as well as meditation and the principles of 'wise' living, according to yogic philosophy, to keep our minds and bodies healthy, treat any illnesses that do occur and – above all – to promote a long and healthy life.

One of the unique benefits of Ayurveda, over and above other systems of medicine, is that it does not simply offer us remedies for ailments. While it can, and does, provide many natural solutions for a catalogue of common health complaints, Ayurveda's fundamental goal is to prevent us from becoming sick in the first place by equipping us with healthy living practices that preserve our health, strengthen our immune system and help us to avoid those diseases to which we are most susceptible.

The definition of health

Health – according to Ayurveda – is when our mind is in a happy state, our senses and motor organs are in good working order, our digestion is strong, tissues well nourished and waste matter (faeces, urine and sweat) is being properly formed and excreted.

Health is achieved by following a diet and lifestyle that maintain the specific balance of our innate mind–body type, and taking steps to manage the impact that the passing of time has on our internal body clock and external environment. In other words, Ayurveda teaches us how, why and when we need to adjust our diet and behaviour to counteract the ageing process, changes in the climate and other environmental factors that can cause health problems.

By tailoring our diets to suit the seasons, for example, we feed our bodies with the right balance of vitamins, minerals and other nutrients needed to protect ourselves from seasonal complaints such as joint problems in autumn/fall, coughs and colds in winter, allergies and skin conditions in summer.

Treating the mind as well as the body

Being a truly holistic system of healthcare, Ayurveda also gives us the tools needed to maintain a healthy, balanced mind via a combination of natural remedies, wise living, methods of mind control involving yoga and meditation, plus unique hands-on therapies such as the soothing treatment of shirodhara, a traditional Ayurvedic remedy for anxiety and depression in which medicated oil is poured continuously over the forehead.

Given that health authorities today believe many illnesses – such as eczema, allergies, hypertension, digestive complaints and weight problems – often have a psychological trigger, these techniques are particularly important for us to understand and put into practice.

Knowledge of Ayurveda is now spreading throughout the developed world because of its ability to promote a healthier lifestyle, as well as its ability to heal or effectively manage many of the lifestyle-related diseases common today, such as diabetes, obesity and stress-related conditions like insomnia, depression and anxiety.

The origins of Ayurveda

The word Ayurveda literally translates as the 'science of life'. Originating in India around 3,000 BC, this complete medical science was developed by ancient Vedic sages. They realized that for the 'goals of human life' to be achieved a person needed to live for at least 100 years! The overall aim of Ayurvedic medicine is, therefore, to empower people to live a long, healthy, happy life and to grow old gracefully.

Since its birth some 5,000 years ago, the wisdom of Ayurveda has not only survived but has had a profound influence on many other healthcare systems including those of ancient Egypt, Syria, Persia and traditional Chinese medicine. Elements of Ayurvedic practice can even be seen in some of the methods used today by modern medicine. The origins of plastic surgery, for instance, can be traced back to one of the key Ayurvedic texts. Written around 3,000 BC, the Susruta Samhita details precisely how to repair wounds to the nose and ears by removing skin from the backs of the arm and suturing it into place.

The first known example of an oral vaccination has its roots in Ayurveda. Every summer, for many thousands of years, Indians have taken a concoction of cow's milk, curd, urine and other natural by-products to promote 'good' bacteria in the gut, helping to protect them from parasites and other acquired diseases.

The ancient Ayurvedic sages also understood the role of good hygiene in disease prevention, realizing that certain viruses and bacteria are transmitted by touch. This legacy can be seen in many of the cultural practices that survive among Indian communities to this day. The traditional Indian welcome of Namaste, for example, where the palms of a person's hands are pressed together in greeting, specifically avoids person-to-person contact. In India it is also common practice to visit the relatives of a dead person only after 11 days have elapsed, allowing time for any contagious bacteria or viruses to die. Even the concept of 'untouchability' promoted by the Indian caste system, while flawed, appears to have its origins in the desire to maintain good hygiene and so avoid disease. The deadly anthrax virus was prevalent among tanners and those handling animal carcasses, hence they became known as the 'untouchables'.

The relevance of Ayurveda today

Today, the Ayurvedic approach to diet – as a way of promoting good health and preventing illness – is mirrored by the advice of nutritionists and other health professionals. The traditional Asian diet is rich in complex carbohydrates, such as rice, as well as fresh vegetables, pulses, seeds and nuts, a combination now widely accepted to be the cornerstones of a balanced and nutritious diet.

So, is this ancient system of traditional medicine really useful for people living a contemporary 'Western' lifestyle?

More than 5,000 years ago, the founders of Ayurveda recognized that people living in overcrowded and polluted environments stripped of nature have a higher risk of disease. Today, health experts agree that the vast majority of the illnesses prevalent in our society are due to inadequate diet, lack of exercise and the stresses of modern life. Urban living, convenience foods and advances in technology are all taking their toll on our day-to-day health.

By following the principles of Ayurveda, we can create a diet and lifestyle, tailored to suit our specific constitutional type, which actively promotes a healthy mind and body, protecting us from common health problems while managing the impact our environment and internal body clock have on our mental and physical wellbeing.

Ayurveda's vast pharmacopoeia of herbal and mineral remedies gives us the ability to treat many of the diseases common in the world today naturally, safely and effectively. It also enables us to manage health issues that occur at different stages of life such as fertility problems, symptoms of the menopause, arthritis and senile dementia.

Right now, there is a surge in demand for traditional medicines and alternative therapies throughout the modern world. More and more people are seeking natural, back-to-basics solutions to health concerns and taking steps to actively improve their health, preserve a youthful appearance and engender a sense of wellbeing. Many are also aiming to relieve chronic conditions, such as back pain and skin complaints, which are often resistant to modern medicine.

As a result, the quality and range of authentic Ayurvedic remedies available to us is increasing rapidly, as are the number of well-qualified practitioners. Ayurveda is a profound and complex science. While there is much you can do yourself to improve your overall health, it is important to know who to consult should more serious health problems arise. With this in mind, a list of leading industry associations you can contact to find a good Ayurvedic practitioner in your area is provided at the end of this book, together with recommended suppliers of authentic Ayurvedic herbs and remedies.

Simple truths to keep in mind

It is hoped that by now you are gaining a sense of the real benefits, adopting an Ayurvedic way of life can deliver. Before you read on, however, it is worth keeping in mind the following simple truths:

- There are no 'quick fixes' in Ayurveda. It is a way of life rather than a short-term medical intervention. Like anything in life, to reap the rewards you must be committed and consistent in your approach. It takes time and sustained effort for positive results to be achieved.

- We are what we eat! Food is one of the most potent medicines known to man and the foundation of any Ayurvedic regimen. However, its benefits are achieved only by sustained and appropriate use over time. This book gives you the tools needed to help identify the types of food best suited to your particular mind–body type, as well as advice on healthy eating practices.

- Everyone is different! There is no panacea for all, which is why one man's poison is another's elixir. The wisdom of Ayurveda lies in its realization that every one of us has a unique constitution that must be kept in balance for a healthy mind and body. While there are some universal truths for healthy living, as this book will explain, we also need to personalize our diet and lifestyle to suit our own specific mind–body type and the environment in which we live. In Chapter 5 you will find a diagnostic tool to help you identify your basic mind–body type and develop a regimen tailored to your specific needs.

- Self-awareness is the key to success. Keep a diary tracking the changes you make to your diet and lifestyle and their impact on your mental and physical wellbeing. This will help you to stay motivated, confirm what works best for you and identify any substances or activities you need to avoid.

02

the core philosophy

In this chapter you will learn:
- about the five elements
- why every substance can be a medicine or toxin
- the role of the three doshas
- the concept of a unique mind–body type
- the importance of the 20 qualities.

A 'back-to-basics' approach

If you have touched on Ayurvedic philosophy before, chances are you are confused or at the very least accept that this is a profound and complex school of thought.

In this book, we are going to keep it simple and focus on the basic principles you need to grasp in order to apply Ayurvedic wisdom to your everyday life without delay. This means we won't go too deeply into fundamental theories about the meaning and causes of life according to Ayurveda. In Appendix 3 you will find recommended texts for further reading should you wish to explore this ancient philosophy in more depth.

The language of Ayurveda is Sanskrit. Some basic Sanskrit terms are introduced in this chapter and used throughout the rest of the book as you need to be familiar with them. As a general rule, however, the use of Sanskrit is kept to a minimum so you can absorb the key concepts without getting bogged down in the language! In Appendix 4 you will find a glossary of all the Sanskrit terms used.

The five elements (panchamahabhutas)

Ayurvedic philosophy on the creation of life, and its approach to the causes, prevention and treatment of any illness, hinges on the five elements or building blocks of life. In Sanskrit these are known as the 'panchamahabhutas'.

This philosophy teaches us that every substance in the universe, whether animate or inanimate, is composed of the same five subtle elements – ether, air, fire, water and earth.

Every substance can be a medicine or poison

Being made up of exactly the same elements, man and nature are are inextricably linked. Any substance – such as a type of food or natural remedy – can therefore be a medicine or poison depending on how it is used. Here are some simple examples:

- In moderation, dairy products are a vital source of saturated fats and calcium. Consumed in excess, however, they can cause congestion, increasing the risk of conditions such as cholesterolaemia and heart disease.

- Honey has many healing properties but must be used correctly. A natural sweetener, it is also a powerful digestive aid, cardio tonic and is useful in respiratory complaints because its dry qualities scrape phlegm and mucus from the respiratory channels. When heated to temperatures of 40 degrees or above, however, honey becomes 'toxic' and blocks the microvessels of the body.

- For thousands of years, Ayurvedic doctors have used purified mercury to treat digestive problems such as colitis and diarrhoea and to strengthen immunity, safely and effectively. When properly processed this originally toxic substance has powerful healing properties. While this is an extreme example, and the Ayurvedic remedies available to us do not contain mercury, it helps to illustrate the point that all substances can be therapeutic if properly applied.

Understanding the five elements and how they work

To understand the concept of the panchamahabhutas (five elements), try not to interpret them too literally, i.e. not as a physical clod of earth or puff of air. Instead, think of them as analogies for the subtle building blocks and catalysts of life responsible for all physical matter as well as psychological and biochemical functions of the mind and body. For instance, energy – represented by air and ether – is needed for us to move our limbs, for our senses to function and for the process of respiration. The fire element drives all our biochemical functions such as digestion and the transformation of waste. Earth and water are the basis of all physical matter, liquid or solid, such as our muscles, bones, blood and plasma.

Modern science tells us that all living matter is composed of nitrogen, hydrogen, carbon and oxygen, and that solar and sound energy are the catalysts required to convert these chemical compounds into life. While it is extremely important not to justify Ayurvedic principles according to different scientific philosophies – as the efficacy of any system of medicine depends on its theories and practices remaining intact – these chemical compounds and catalytic converters are all present in the building blocks of life identified by Ayurveda, as can be seen from the following table.

Panchamahabhuta	Chemical composition	Biochemical action	Sensory function
Ether	Sound energy	A catalyst for biochemical actions	Hearing
Air	Nitrogen, oxygen and other minor gases	When nitrogen is added to carbon and H^2O, amino acids and proteins are formed	Touch
Fire	Solar radiation	A catalyst for biochemical actions, e.g. digestion	Sight
Water	Hydrogen + oxygen (H_2O)	Combined with carbon, these chemicals convert into fats and carbohydrates	Taste (unless water is present we cannot taste)
Earth	Carbon	As above	Smell

You will notice that, in this table, each of the five elements is related to a specific sensory function, that is, hearing, sight, smell, touch and taste. This is important for you to understand. As will be explained fully in the next chapter, a common cause of illness is the unhealthy use of our five senses. This table helps to explain how misusing any one of our senses of perception has the power to affect our core being and therefore cause disease. Consider, for example, how listening to extremely loud music can damage your hearing and how straining your eyes at a computer screen for hours on end eventually impairs your vision.

The three doshas (vata, pitta, kapha)

The Sanskrit term 'dosha' is one you may recognize. It is probably the best-known principle of Ayurveda today and the cornerstone of its method of diagnosis, disease prevention and treatment. The fundamental goal of Ayurvedic practice –

whether aiming to prevent or treat an illness – is to maintain or restore your own specific and innate doshic balance via a combination of diet, lifestyle and natural remedies.

So what are the doshas? Essentially, the five elements form the basis of three biological humours or doshas:

- 'Vata' is composed of air and ether
- 'Pitta' is composed of the fire element with some water
- 'Kapha' is composed of earth and water.

These three doshas govern all the psychobiological functions and physical features of our mind and body, including our appearance, mental state, memory, digestive capacity, processes of waste elimination, individual likes and dislikes, as well as dictating which diseases we are most susceptible to.

Every one of us has a totally unique combination of Vata, Pitta and Kapha. This concept of Ayurveda is known as 'prakriti' and translates as our unique mind–body type or personal constitution. When our particular doshic combination is in balance we enjoy good health; any imbalance, however, kick starts the process of disease causation.

To understand how the doshas work – and be able to identify our own specific doshic constitution and how to keep this in balance – we need to know the core qualities and functions of Vata, Pitta and Kapha, as well as their inter-relationship with the passing of time, such as the various stages of life and changing seasons.

Vata = air and ether

Vata is arguably the most influential dosha. This is because it governs all movement and activates our neurological and biological functions. The word 'Vata' means 'to move, spread, flow', which helps us to understand how it works. Without the flow of Vata, the other two doshas (Pitta and Kapha) are unable to function. Most health problems therefore have some form of Vata imbalance at their root.

Being composed of air and ether, Vata is invisible, but it is the power behind all the 'actions' of our minds and bodies, including the movement of our limbs, respiration, waste elimination processes, speech and neurological functions. It also controls our sense of hearing and touch. Without Vata we, quite literally, lose the ability to think, breathe or move properly.

The specific qualities of Vata, like those of air and ether, are cold, dry, light, rough, mobile, subtle (minute), clear and astringent. When Vata is balanced a person tends to feel creative, vibrant and dynamic. When Vata is out of balance, however, a person may experience feelings of fearfulness and anxiety due to the abundance of cold, light, mobile qualities in the mind and body.

Vata occupies the spaces in the body such as the large intestine, joints, ears and head. As a result, people with a high level of Vata dosha in their constitution are prone to constipation, cracking joints, tinnitus and mental health problems.

Each of the doshas prevails during a particular time of life, which helps to explain why we are susceptible to certain diseases at a certain age. Vata is the dosha that dominates in old age, taking control at around the age of 55 and causing conditions such as the menopause, brittle bones and arthritis.

In Chapter 5 we will look more closely at the qualities of Vata dosha, how these translate into physical and mental traits, plus some simple guidelines for keeping Vata in balance.

Pitta = the fire element

Being largely composed of the fire element, the word Pitta actually means 'to cook'. This dosha is present in all the liquids of the body, such as the blood and digestive fluids, so also has some water in its composition.

Pitta governs all the metabolic and biochemical functions in the body and mind. Amino acids and digestive enzymes can be seen as the actions of Pitta dosha. As well as being responsible for the digestion of food, Pitta digests our ideas and is responsible, therefore, for our intellectual capacity and powers of discrimination. It also controls body temperature, which explains why people of a strongly Pitta constitution sweat easily and are prone to fever.

Pitta dominates between the ages of 20 and 55 – the stage in our lives when we need to be most productive in professional and family terms. It is the Pitta quality that gives us the drive and determination to achieve.

Pitta is located predominantly in the small intestine, blood, liver, skin and eyes, which is why any Pitta imbalance usually manifests as digestive upsets, blood disorders, skin problems and poor vision. Its particular qualities are hot, sharp, slightly oily, liquid, quick-moving, sour and pungent.

Kapha = earth and water

Composed of earth and water, Kapha translates as 'to stick'. It is the dosha that literally binds the body together and is also responsible for our senses of taste and smell.

Essentially, Kapha is the substance of the physical body, that which gives it shape and cohesion. Its primary role is growth and ongoing nourishment of the mind and body, which helps to explain why this dosha predominates during childhood, the period of growth and development. It also explains why people with a Kapha constitution have a strong, healthy immune system and loads of stamina.

Located predominantly in the upper body, namely the head, chest, heart and lungs, imbalances of Kapha dosha are the root cause of all mucus-related conditions and congestion within the body, such as lung complaints, coughs and colds and coronary heart disease. This is because the core qualities of Kapha dosha are cold, moist, heavy, oily, slow, smooth, firm, sticky and sweet.

Together the three doshas govern all the psychobiological actions of the body, with Kapha controlling the anabolic (building) processes such as cellular renewal, Pitta regulating our biochemical functions and Vata managing all the catabolic actions such as the breaking down of tissues in the body.

The relationship between the doshas and time

The functions of the doshas are also inherently linked to the passing of time. We have already noted that each dosha rules over a particular stage of life, but they also take control at certain times of day and year, as the next table illustrates.

Controlling dosha	Time of day	Time of year
Vata	2a.m.–6a.m. 2p.m.–6p.m.	Autumn and early winter
Kapha	6a.m.–10a.m. 6p.m.–10p.m.	Late winter and spring
Pitta	10a.m.–2p.m. 10p.m.–2a.m.	Summer

This helps to explain why we are at our mental peak and our digestion is at its strongest between the hours of 10a.m. and 2p.m.

when fiery Pitta is at its height; why we tend to wind down after 6p.m., when sluggish Kapha takes control; and why, when we are anxious, insomnia often strikes in the early hours of morning, when Vata rules.

In Chapter 7 we will look more closely at the relationship between the doshas and time and how we can use this knowledge to create a healthy daily and seasonal routine for ourselves.

Qualities of the mind

Vata, Pitta and Kapha doshas are mirrored by three mental qualities, Sattva, Rajas and Tamas. To avoid confusion we will not look at these in great detail; however, you need to grasp the basic principles.

Sattva is the ideal mental state but it is very rare. It can be likened to the supreme state of enlightenment or clarity that comes with regular practice of deep meditation. Examples of Sattvic behaviour include acting with self-control, acquiring knowledge and using our powers of discrimination. When we achieve a Sattvic state of mind we feel happy, calm, light and content.

Rajas and Tamas are known as the 'mind doshas' because they have the power to cause disease. While we need a healthy dose of both Rajas and Tamas for our minds to have their full range of cognitive abilities, an excess of either one can lead to mental health problems. Aggravated Rajas results in an overactive, anxious mind, anger and irritability, while too much Tamas triggers despondency, laziness and ignorance. Rajas and Tamas can be increased by negative desires and emotions such as lust, greed and envy as well as by stress.

The mind swings between these three mental states like a pendulum and we need all three states to attain our goals in life. Leadership and dynamism are derived, for example, from Rajas; Sattva helps us to think clearly and retain knowledge; Tamas enables us to relax and to sleep.

So – while we need Rajas and Tamas to be active – we also need to learn methods of mind control that can prevent these mind doshas from becoming too dominant and that promote a more Sattvic state of mind. In the next chapter we will look at the methods of self-control and ethical behaviour we can use to protect our mental equilibrium and avoid problems such as stress, insomnia, anxiety and depression.

The concept of prakriti (unique mind–body type)

Ayurveda teaches us that every one of us has a unique mind and body type or 'prakriti', which is formed at the point of our conception. It consists of a totally individual combination of the three doshas – Vata, Pitta and Kapha – and is determined by our parent's own particular constitutional types, state of mind and lifestyle at the time when the sperm and ova fused to create us. For example, if our mother and father were predominantly Pitta prakriti themselves, but we were conceived during a period of uncertainty and anxiety in their lives or relationship, the chances are that both Pitta and Vata will be strongly represented in our own constitution and that features of both these doshas will be apparent in our appearance, behaviour and susceptibility to disease.

This concept of prakriti – or a unique constitutional make-up – shares a common theme with the modern scientific principle of DNA, which is defined as a unique genetic code or blueprint.

According to Ayurveda, there are seven possible types of prakriti:

- Vata
- Pitta
- Kapha
- Vata-Pitta
- Vata-Kapha
- Pitta-Kapha
- Vata-Pitta-Kapha (an equal balance of all three doshas; this type is extremely rare).

In each case all three doshas are always present, but generally one or more will predominate, giving rise to certain psychological and physical traits/behaviour.

The following points will help you to grasp the concept of prakriti more clearly:

- No two people are exactly the same, which is why this book will teach you how to diagnose your own specific mind–body type and develop a healthy way of life to suit your needs.

- Each of the three doshas is present in our make-up, but usually one or more will predominate. This specific combination in an individual is known as their prakriti.

- The aim of Ayurveda is to preserve our own particular doshic balance (prakriti), which is established at the point of our conception. Maintaining this specific balance ensures that we stay healthy.

- Being in balance does *not* mean that we each need to have an equal proportion of Vata, Pitta and Kapha dosha to be healthy. If this were the case, we would all look and act the same! Our doshic idiosyncrasies are what make us individuals. It explains why some people are talented artists and others good at maths; why some of us are well organized and others more haphazard; why some people gain weight easily and others do not. It also explains why there is no one diet, system of exercise or way of life to suit all.

- Our prakriti is maintained by following a diet and pattern of behaviour that preserve this innate constitutional balance.

- Health problems occur whenever this natural state of balance is upset. This 'upset' may be due to us eating the wrong foods, taking insufficient exercise, or environmental influences such as a change of season. In Ayurveda this state of imbalance is called 'vikriti'.

In Chapter 5, you will learn how to identify your natural constitutional type (prakriti) as well as any imbalances (vikriti) that may have developed due to your diet, lifestyle and/or environment.

The role of the gunas (20 qualities)

The common denominator, or link, between all the concepts outlined so far – the five elements, doshas, prakriti and vikriti – is that they are all made up of certain qualities. Hot, cold, oily, dry, rough, smooth, for example, are terms with which you are now becoming familiar. It makes sense that every substance is made of certain qualities. In Ayurveda, these are called the 'gunas' and their application and impact on the mind and body is the basis of its approach to health management, as will be explained further. For the moment, let's just familiarize ourselves with the 20 qualities that form the basis of all substances and their effects on the body. They can be divided into ten pairs of opposites, as shown in the following table.

Quality	Impact	Opposing quality	Impact
Light	Lightens or reduces	Heavy	Nourishes
Hot	Expands/opens up	Cold	Blocks/arrests
Moist	Binds or sticks	Dry	Dries out
Rough	Scrapes	Smooth	Heals
Liquid	Dilutes	Solid	Concentrates
Quick	Eliminates/evacuates	Slow	Alleviates/soothes
Tiny	Opens	Large	Closes/fills
Mobile	Activates/facilitates	Static	Holds
Slimy	Envelops	Non-slimy	Cleanses
Soft	Softens	Hard	Hardens

An excess or deficiency of any one of these qualities in the body can lead to health problems. For example, a person who regularly eats too much heavy, nourishing food will increase the level of Kapha dosha in their body (itself composed of sweet, heavy qualities), leading to weight gain and even obesity. Eating too much hot, spicy food will aggravate Pitta dosha, causing problems such as acid indigestion, heartburn and even ulcers. Overindulging in dry, cold foods can upset Vata dosha, leading to complaints such as constipation.

Once you accept that our prakriti is actually no more than a particular blend of these 20 qualities, in varying proportions, you can begin to appreciate how the Ayurvedic system of medicine works. We are all constantly exposed to internal and external forces which have the power to alter the specific balance of these qualities in our minds and bodies, such as the food we eat, changes in seasons and the ageing process.

In the next chapter we will explore how these qualities can be used to protect our health and heal common complaints.

Summary

You have learned a lot of new information in this chapter, so let's summarize the key points you need to keep in mind to move forward.

1 Everyone has a totally unique mind–body type, composed of a particular combination of the three doshas, Vata, Pitta and Kapha.

2 Health is maintained when this specific balance of the three doshas is preserved via a personalized programme of diet, lifestyle activities and other healthy living practices.

3 An increase or decrease of any one of the 20 qualities from which our minds and bodies are composed can upset our doshic balance, leading to health problems.

03

the causes of disease and how to avoid them

In this chapter you will learn:
- that like substances increase their like
- common causes of disease and ways to avoid them
- that good digestion is the key to good health
- about the immunity factor.

How to achieve good health

Health occurs when the doshas are in their natural state of balance. This allows our digestion and metabolism to work properly, so our tissues are well fed, the channels of the body are free from obstruction and waste matter is properly formed and excreted. This also ensures a strong immune system and happy state of mind. It is achieved by wholesome use of the mind, our senses of perception and the physical body, and by knowing the causes of disease, the ways to avoid them and how to treat an illness if it does occur.

Ayurveda teaches us that there are three basic causes of ill health, all of which we can avoid by adopting a way of life in harmony with our particular environment, stage of life and constitutional type. They are:

- the impact of time
- unhealthy use of the mind and intellect
- abuse of the five senses (taste, touch, hearing, sight and smell).

Each of these factors has the power to upset our doshic balance. Once this happens, the fabric of our system begins to malfunction.

The law of similarity and dissimilarity

Before we analyse these causes in detail, we need to get to grips with the key to disease causation, prevention and treatment according to Ayurveda. It lies in the law of similarity and dissimilarity, or 'samanya vishesha' in Sanskrit. This teaches us that like substances increase their like and dissimilar substances reduce their opposing qualities in the mind and body. A dosha, for example, is increased by experiences and substances (such as food and weather conditions) that are similar to it and decreased by its opposites. This explains why Vata dosha – which has cold and dry qualities – is increased by cold, dry weather; why the fiery nature of Pitta is aggravated by hot, spicy foods; and why Kapha – itself predominantly heavy, cold and oily in quality – is increased by heavy, mucus-producing foods such as ice cream, as well as by cold, damp weather.

According to this law, Vata can therefore be reduced by substances with opposing qualities, such as, warm, oily, nourishing foods, Pitta with cool, slightly drying substances and Kapha by warm, light and drying qualities.

As a result, all the therapies used to promote good health or treat an illness in Ayurveda – be they foods, natural medicines, exercise routines, methods of mind control or hands-on healing techniques – are defined and applied according to their core properties (hot, cold, dry, oily, etc.) and their related effect on the doshas and functions of the mind and body. For example, fresh ginger root, which is warming by nature, is used to pacify chilly Vata dosha and build digestive fire. Cooling foods such as ghee (clarified butter) and peppermint tea take the heat out of Pitta. High-impact exercise, which is stimulating and energizing, helps to counteract the heavy, indolent nature of Kapha dosha.

This principle is nothing new. When you think about it we already apply it to our everyday lives. When it is cold, we wear warm clothes, we quench our thirst with liquids and moisten dry skin with nourishing oils. To lose weight we cut down on sweet, fatty foods; to soothe an overactive mind we take time out to relax or practise calming therapies such as deep breathing, meditation and yoga. These common practices are all examples of samanya vishesha in action.

Now let us look at the common causes of disease. Once we know what they are, we can *act* to avoid them.

How time influences our health

Time is a common cause of ill health because its impact is constant, unstoppable and profound. When we ignore the rigours of time, we are ignoring the rhythm of nature of which we are all part. Consider how, as time passes, the fabric of our minds and bodies alters. Our skin becomes drier, our bones more brittle, joints less flexible and our senses less acute. Consider how changes in the season bring with them specific pathogens, bacteria and infections, such as influenza, and how eating too fast can cause gas, bloating and indigestion.

Time is relentless. To remain healthy we must counteract its effects through the foods we eat and the way we behave.

The stages of life or ageing process

In Chapter 2 we noted how each of the doshas prevails during a particular time of life. Kapha governs our childhood, which is why up until our late teens we tend to need more sleep and are prone to congestive problems such as coughs, colds and allergies. Pitta rules between the ages of 20 and 55. At this time we are at our most dynamic but are also susceptible to conditions such as 'burn out', peptic ulcers and hypertension due to the intensity of Pitta qualities in the mind and body. Vata takes control in later life. It explains why in old age we sleep less and are prone to degenerative disorders such as arthritis and Alzheimer's.

By understanding the impact of time we start to appreciate why it is so important for us to tailor our diets and lifestyles to suit our time of life. In youth, for example, our bodies are capable of – and indeed thrive on – high-impact exercise, whereas in old age we benefit from more gentle pursuits, such as yoga, which boost circulation and flexibility without straining our joints and bones.

In Part Two of this book we will explore the types of diet and behaviour we need to follow to counteract the effect of age on our minds and bodies.

How the seasons influence health

Changes in the season bring different weather conditions as well as various disease-causing organisms. While we can't control the weather, or the prevalence of viruses and bacteria, we can take steps to protect ourselves by dressing warmly in winter, increasing our fluid intake in summer and eating seasonally fresh foods to build our natural immunity. These are all practical examples of how we already take timely action to manage the impact of the seasons and avoid becoming sick.

Just as the stages of life are governed by a particular dosha, so too are the seasons. The moist, slightly warmer conditions of spring liquefy and aggravate Kapha; in the heat of summer Pitta is increased; while the dry, windy and cold weather of autumn/fall and early winter excites Vata dosha.

Whatever your constitutional type, these qualities in the mind and body will increase according to the time of year, but you will only become sick if they reach excessive levels. It stands to reason, therefore, that if your constitution is Pitta predominant, you need to take particular care to avoid heat-increasing foods and activities in summer. Similarly, if you are a Kapha type of person keep mucus-producing foods such as dairy and wheat to a minimum in spring. In early winter, Vata types need to keep warm and eat plenty of nourishing foods, such as soups and stews.

In Part Two of this book you will learn how to identify your mind–body type, as well as how to adjust your diet and lifestyle to suit changes in the season and stay healthy.

Listening to our internal body clock

Ignoring the demands of our internal body clock – the timely calls of nature – by suppressing natural urges such as thirst, hunger, sexual desire and sleep, can also damage our health.

If, due to our busy lifestyles, we continually put off going to the toilet for instance, constipation is likely to result! By the time we feel thirsty our bodies are already dehydrated, which is why it is so important to drink at least two litres of water a day. Similarly, we need to eat when we are hungry and at regular times of the day. Skipping meals upsets our digestion, as does eating before the previous meal has been digested.

Sleep is also vital for our wellbeing. Lack of sleep reduces our IQ and compromises our immunity, allowing mental and physical toxins to build. A short catnap of 10–15 minutes in the day is good for both Vata and Pitta types and helps our bodies to recover from long-distance travel and late nights. Kapha types, however, should avoid sleeping in the day as it slows their already sluggish metabolism.

All of these time-related factors can upset our natural equilibrium. This is why Ayurveda puts such great emphasis on adopting a disciplined, daily routine to suit our specific environment, time of life and constitutional type. In Chapter 7 you will learn more about how to live in harmony with your inner body clock, the seasons, times of day and stages of life.

The power of the mind

Once we accept that our mind and body are inextricably linked, it makes sense that our thoughts and emotions have the potential to affect not only our state of mind but also our physical wellbeing. Every thought and emotion actually triggers a biochemical reaction within the body, which is why keeping our minds healthy is such a vital part of preserving our overall health. Just as positive emotions boost energy levels and our enthusiasm for life, negative emotions – such as anxiety, guilt, envy, fear and anger – deplete our system and can trigger many health problems such as depression.

Stress and disease

Stress is a common cause of illness in the modern world. There are many triggers, our work–life balance, relationships with friends and family or simply pushing our bodies too far with late nights, alcohol and inadequate diets. Whatever the reason, stress is thought to cause many problems, including high blood pressure, asthma, anxiety and even heart disease.

Depending on which of the doshas is upset, stress manifests itself in different ways. If Vata increases, fear, anxiety, insomnia, feelings of isolation and loss of appetite usually follow. In Pitta aggravation we may suffer from heartburn, hypertension or ulcerative colitis, while Kapha types just try to eat their way out of trouble!

The key to managing stress is self-knowledge and awareness. We may not be able to alter the pressures around us but if we know our mind–body type – and use it to identify our personal hot spots – we can reduce its impact on our health by adapting our diet, lifestyle and mental approach and through the use of rejuvenating natural therapies.

A unique feature of Ayurvedic medicine is 'rasayana' or rejuvenation therapy. Only Ayurveda has a specific branch of medicine dedicated to building our core immunity factor on a psychological and physical level. It is a tool we can build into our everyday lives to overcome the impact of conditions such as stress, and one which we will examine in greater detail in the next few chapters.

Negative thoughts and emotions

Ayurveda sees negative emotions as mental toxins. As well as upsetting the mind they have a direct impact on our physical state. Fear, for example, is often accompanied by tummy upsets! Seeing negative thoughts and emotions as mental toxins can help us find ways to eliminate these disease-causing agents. In the same way that we detoxify our physical body, we can detoxify our mind. The secret lies in the practice of mind control, that is, in our ability to capture, rationalize and replace these thoughts with healthier, more positive perceptions.

Here are some simple ways to eliminate mental toxins:

• Apply the principles of samanya vishesha to your mind. If you are feeling fearful, think of situations that make you feel safe and secure. If you are angry, try meditating on a peaceful scene or situation.

- Don't bury your emotions. Instead, recognize them and take steps to resolve them. If you are having relationship problems, for instance, ignoring them won't make them go away – you need to act!
- Use your intelligence to measure the quality and accuracy of your thoughts. Are they a valid response, a misperception or an over-reaction?
- Talk to a friend or a therapist. Sharing your worries with others helps to cleanse the mind of negative thoughts and to correct faulty perceptions.
- Practise pranayama (controlled breathing techniques) and meditation (see Chapters 7 and 8).

Doing what's right!

One of the great pearls of Ayurvedic wisdom is its focus on 'wise' living. By setting ourselves wholesome standards of behaviour and ethics, we avoid many negative emotions such as guilt and fear. Yoga – which is an integral part of Ayurveda – teaches us that 'right conduct' is the path to peace of mind and therefore a key method of achieving good health. Some everyday examples of judicious living are:

- non-violence in our thoughts, words and deeds
- truthfulness
- cleanliness of mind and body, through the purity of the foods we eat and our standards of personal hygiene, for example
- contentment; being satisfied with our inner self
- practising self-restraint.

Wise living and the environment

The need for wise conduct doesn't just apply to ourselves – we can see its impact, or lack of it, all around us. It has the power to positively or negatively affect our surroundings and therefore our collective and individual health. Consider how commercial activities around the world are polluting and denuding the environment and are linked to a surge in health problems such as asthma.

Our personal and collective good health depends on the preservation of our environment, which is one very good reason to select consumer products wisely, by favouring those which are ecofriendly, organic and ethically produced.

Knowing better!

Wise living also means listening to that 'inner voice', the one that tells you when a particular path is detrimental to your health. If you know that eating lots of bread and pasta makes you constipated, or putting off an unwanted task will only prey on your mind, why do it!

When we listen to our inner voice, exercise self-control and avoid patterns of behaviour that we know are counter-productive, we can actually improve our self-esteem as well as our overall health.

Exercise is a good example of an activity that we all know is good for us but which we often avoid! Lack of exercise is the root of many diseases common today, such as obesity, heart problems and diabetes. The trick is to find a form of exercise that suits you, whether it's taking a brisk walk, climbing the escalators everyday on your way to work, going to the gym, practising yoga or simply doing some vigorous housework!

Abusing our senses

How we use or abuse our sense of taste, touch, smell, sight and hearing actually affects our health! It is said that the average man has a daily quota of 7,000 words, women more than 21,000 words. Once this quota is reached we are 'talked out'. While this is an amusing bit of trivia it also demonstrates that our senses have limited use.

Like our bodies, our senses need a balance of wholesome exercise and rest. As with all our mental and physical functions, a biochemical action occurs every time we use our senses, which means over-, under- or misuse has a direct impact on our core being. In Chapter 2 we learned that each sense is linked to one of the five elements; this helps us to understand why sensory abuse can affect our overall physical and mental wellbeing.

Over-, under- and misuse of the senses

Straining your eyes can cause headaches (overuse); getting water in your ears can lead to hearing problems (misuse); while lack of sunlight can trigger despondency and lethargy (underuse). Sensory overload is a big problem today and a common cause of stress due to the steady assault of e-mails, mobile phone calls, TV, noise and air pollution, for example.

Using our senses wisely

Just like the rest of our body, we need to use our senses wisely and give them healthy doses of exercise. Positive forms of sensory exercise include aromatherapy (smell), massage (touch), listening to soothing classical music or mantras (sound) and eating wholesome foods which are fresh, in season and free from preservatives (taste).

We also need to find space in our busy lives to 'take time out' and rest our senses. Yoga is actually designed to 'still' the mind and the senses, rather than simply promoting flexibility and muscle tone. By concentrating on a certain posture or pattern of breathing, meditating on a mantra or visual image, we can detach ourselves from our senses, giving them time to rest and ourselves the chance to get in touch with our inner being which is the key to tranquillity and wellbeing. In Chapters 7 and 8 you will find examples of therapeutic yoga practices to cultivate.

The importance of good digestion

Whatever the cause of an illness, an invariable and critical step in its development is a faulty digestive system, according to Ayurveda. When our digestive capacity is compromised we lose our ability to build healthy tissues and nourish our immune system allowing disease to take hold.

'Agni' is the term used in Ayurveda to describe our digestive fire and metabolic processes. In Western medical terms it dovetails with the principle of digestive enzymes and amino acids, as well as the catabolic (deconstructing) and anabolic (building) processes which feed our tissues and eliminate waste.

What and how we eat changes according to the seasons. Physical, mental and emotional factors all have the power to upset agni and allow undigested food substances called 'ama' to build up in the gastro-intestinal (GI) tract. Ama is a highly toxic, heavy, sticky substance, which coats the GI tract before invading our tissues and impeding metabolic functions. The result is malnourishment and a breakdown in immunity.

Detecting ama in your system

One of the easiest ways to detect the presence of ama is to check your tongue and stools. Typically, the tongue will have a whitish coating, the stools will be heavy (tending to sink rather than float!), dark, strong smelling and possibly contain some mucus. You may also feel tired, especially after eating, and have symptoms of indigestion such as bloating and wind as well as bad breath.

Three types of faulty digestion

Ayurveda teaches us that there are three types of improper digestion:

1 Erratic digestion (vishamagni) is sometimes quick and sometimes slow and is typical of Vata aggravation. Its symptoms include an irregular appetite, bloating, indigestion, intestinal cramps, constipation and gas. It can be triggered by an erratic routine, eating and sleeping at odd hours of the day and night, for example. You can treat it by including more sweet and pungent flavours in your diet such as fresh ginger root, cumin and fennel, taking Ayurvedic remedies such as Trikatu and Hingvastaka churna before you eat (see Chapter 9) and eating at regular times of the day.

2 Rapid digestion (tikshnagni) is a sign of Pitta aggravation. The excess heat and quick-moving properties inherent in Pitta dosha means we burn up food too quickly, once again leading to malnourishment and debility. Typical symptoms include excessive thirst, frequent or excessive hunger, dry throat, loose stools, low blood sugar levels and a burning sensation in the stomach. You can combat it by increasing the use of mild, sweet flavours in your diet, such as buttermilk and complex carbohydrates which balance blood sugar levels. Useful Ayurvedic remedies include Shatavari (Asparagus racemosus), Guduci (Tinospora cordifolia) and Amalaki (Emblica officinalis). In Chapter 9 you will find more details on these and other common Ayurvedic herbs. Eat small, regular meals and avoid hot spices, fried foods, coffee and alcohol.

3 Sluggish digestion (mandagni) is the principle cause of ama and the root cause of many diseases, including rheumatoid arthritis, diabetes and obesity, according to Ayurveda. It is the most common form of digestive problem today because the typical modern diet is rich in toxins, such as artificial preservatives and substances that are overly processed or hard to digest, like convenience foods, some dairy products and wheat. Use more bitter and pungent flavours in your cooking to combat it, such as fresh ginger root and cinnamon, and adopt a lighter diet. The Ayurvedic remedy, Trikatu, is often used to treat mandagni.

All forms of inadequate digestion result in malabsorption and derangement of one or more doshas, as well as causing upset to the tissues, channels of the body and our ability to properly form and eliminate waste products. Eventually our immunity is impaired, increasing our risk of disease.

Modern medicine sees this process as the fermentation of undigested substances in the gut, which upsets intestinal flora, increasing our risk of infection and disease. It's a concept you may be familiar with.

Keeping your digestion healthy

Good digestion (samagni) is an invariable goal of Ayurvedic medical intervention. To achieve it we must first purge the GI tract and tissues of the body of undigested toxins via a light diet or period of fasting, plus ama-digesting herbal remedies like Trikatu (see Chapter 9). Ideally one of the five methods of detoxification (panchakarma) described in the next chapter is then used to flush deep-rooted toxins from the body. After this, we need to follow a diet and lifestyle suited to our constitution, the seasons and our stage of life. The next few chapters will give you the tools necessary to build these practices into your everyday life.

Protecting our immunity

This is the final piece of the jigsaw in terms of staying healthy and it underlines why good digestion is so important.

According to Ayurvedic wisdom, our immunity is a by-product of each of the seven tissues of the body, particularly our reproductive tissue (shukra dhatu). Once our digestion is impaired these tissues become malnourished, so our body's ability to produce this vital essence – known as ojas – is reduced. The loss of ojas increases our risk of disease. Typical symptoms of poor immunity include weight loss, mental health problems and a general feeling of fatigue and debility. Chronic fatigue syndrome – a condition that has mystified conventional medicine – could be an example of what happens to the body when ojas is depleted.

In terms of qualities, ojas is similar to Kapha dosha in that it is sweet, heavy, oily and cold. This is why Kapha predominant people have such robust constitutions and why Vata types –

whose key qualities are dry, light and astringent and therefore opposite in nature to ojas – are more prone to disease.

In the next couple of chapters we will learn how to strengthen and conserve our natural immunity.

Summary

Let's review the key lessons we have learned in this chapter.

1 Like substances and experiences increase their like, while opposites have a decreasing effect. This law applies to both the causes of disease and their prevention or treatment.

2 The simplest way to stay healthy is to recognize and avoid the common causes of disease by adopting a diet and lifestyle that suits your environment, time of life and constitutional type.

3 Keeping your digestion strong is the key to good health and a robust immune system.

04

traditional methods of healing

In this chapter you will learn:
- the three steps to healing any illness
- the two methods of treatment – pacify or purge
- detoxing the Ayurvedic way
- ways to strengthen your mind and body.

yurveda's approach to treatment and prevention

In this chapter we will look at the methods – in addition to your diet and way of life – that are traditionally used in Ayurveda to treat disease and revitalize the mind and body.

Not all of these are self-healing methods. It is important for us to recognize when an illness can be treated effectively by diet, lifestyle and some simple home remedies and when we need help from of a qualified Ayurvedic doctor or practitioner. Chronic diseases such as diabetes and psoriasis, for example, have deep-rooted pathogenic factors, which require expert knowledge and intensive therapies to be properly managed or even cured. A simple cough or cold, however, can be quite easily treated at home.

Whatever the therapeutic tool, all Ayurvedic treatments hinge on the principle that like substances increase their like and opposites reduce. You need to keep this in mind to fully appreciate Ayurveda's approach to healing.

Three steps for healing disease

Ayurveda teaches us that there are three steps to managing any kind of ill health:

1 Remove the causes.
2 Pacify or purge the body of disease-causing agents.
3 Revitalise the mind and body.

Recognize and remove the causes

Whatever the nature of a disease, the first step is to identify and eliminate the causative factors. If you are a type 2 diabetic or suffering from obesity, for instance, it is important to avoid sweet, fatty foods and a sedentary lifestyle.

In the previous chapter, we looked at the three causes of disease in detail, so you know how to identify them. Use your diary to monitor the foods, behaviour and situations that affect your health positively and negatively. Remember to take into account your age, the seasons, your state of mind and other influences.

If you do start to feel unwell, what preceded this feeling? Stay alert, identify the triggers and then take action to modify your behaviour and eradicate the likely culprits!

Two methods of treatment – pacify or purge

Once you've identified and taken action to remove the causes, there are two ways to treat any disease according to Ayurvedic principles. You can either:

- pacify the condition with foods, natural remedies and therapies that are opposite in nature to the aggravated dosha/qualities of the disease; or
- purge your body of the disease-causing agents through Ayurveda's powerful process of internal cleansing or detoxification known as 'panchakarma' (five methods of purgation).

For either route to work there is an essential first step!

Restoring your digestive fire

In the previous chapter we learned that faulty digestion is a contributing factor in any illness. We must first rekindle our digestive fire so that curative medicines can be fully digested and assimilated. This is why an invariable step in managing any illness is to restore our digestive power to its optimum capacity. To do this we must first cleanse the GI tract of undigested toxins via a process known as 'amapachana' and then restore the digestive fire to its maximum strength, a process known as 'agni deepana' in Sanskrit.

Even if you feel healthy at the moment, the chances are you have ama in your system, because the typical Western diet is so high in processed foods and toxins. The most effective way to eliminate ama is through Ayurveda's five methods of detoxification. Another simple method, available to us all, is to follow one of the fasting regimens given later in this chapter.

Natural remedies that pacify disease

A holistic mix of diet and lifestyle, natural remedies and hands-on healing therapies is used to pacify and heal many common health problems.

If, for instance, you have a heavy cold, following a light diet of freshly cooked vegetables, soups and stews, plus drinking a tea made with hot water and freshly grated ginger root, helps to digest mucus and speed recovery. Trikatu, a traditional Ayurvedic formula of three pungent spices – black pepper, dried ginger and long pepper – can also be used. It is hot and drying in effect as well as having a natural affinity for the lungs and head, making it a superb remedy for winter coughs and colds, breathing problems and allergies. Refer to Chapter 9 for more information on Trikatu and other traditional Ayurvedic remedies mentioned in this section, and consult Appendix 2 for a list of recommended suppliers.

If you suffer from chronic constipation, following a Vata-pacifying diet such as the one given in Chapter 6 and taking Triphala – a blend of three nourishing fruits – can eliminate the problem. Triphala has a mild, purgative action on the GI tract due to its lubricating qualities. It is a powerful natural remedy for chronic constipation and, unlike most conventional laxatives, can be used safely for prolonged periods of time. It is also a natural rejuvenator, which means it will boost your immunity while healing your constipation.

In Chapters 9 and 10 we will look at some of the herbal remedies that are widely available and how they can be used to pacify complaints such as irritable bowel syndrome, indigestion and symptoms of the menopause.

Hands-on therapies that pacify disease

A variety of traditional, hands-on Ayurvedic therapies are now more widely available. They are often used, together with diet and natural remedies, to heal the symptoms of a disease. It helps to know what they are and when to use them, although they usually need to be given by a qualified practitioner.

Shirodhara (see figure 1) is a sublime therapy used to treat nervous disorders due to aggravated Vata dosha, such as tension, depression, stress and insomnia, as well as conditions due to aggravated Pitta dosha, such as high blood pressure and hypertension. A medicated oil is selected to counteract the qualities of the specific doshic imbalance, warmed and poured continuously onto the third eye (forehead) to soothe the mind and body. Its effect is similar to the profound sense of peace which can usually only be achieved through regular meditation.

Other therapies involving the application of medicated oils to the head include **shiropichu** and **shirobasti**. Both are commonly used to treat nervous disorders and other complaints, so you may well come across them.

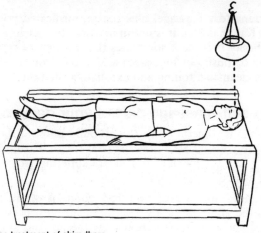

figure 1 The treatment of shirodhara

Pinda sweda is a useful home remedy. A hot bolus of healing herbs and spices is used to relieve muscular pain, joint problems and degenerative conditions such as osteoporosis and arthritis, which are Vata-related conditions. Simply fill a tea towel with 250gm each of ginger powder and ajwain powder (available from most good Asian foods stores) and tie it securely to create a bolus. Heat this carefully over an iron or hotplate and apply it to the affected area in a gentle pounding motion until the pain is relieved.

Kati basti involves the localized application of warm, medicated oils or herbal decoctions to the lower back and is used to treat backpain and other degenerative conditions. This therapy eases any tension in the lower spine and strengthens bone tissue in this region.

Netra tarpana cleanses, nourishes and strengthens the muscles around the eyes. A ring of dough is built up around each eye socket and then filled with medicated oils or milks. It is used to improve vision, reduce inflammation and treat headaches, tension, glaucoma and cataracts.

Therapeutic massage, either oily or dry, is used in Ayurveda, depending on the doshic imbalance. Traditionally two masseurs will work on the body in synchronized strokes.

• Abhyanga (oily massage) treats Vata and Pitta problems. Generous quantities of medicated oil are systematically applied to the body and massaged from head to toe.

- Udvartana (dry massage) uses coarse, medicated powders to pacify Kapha dosha. It is useful in conditions such as cellulite and obesity because it stimulates the channels of circulation, helping to flush out blockages and toxins from the body, as well as cleansing, toning and exfoliating the skin.

Making self-massage part of your daily routine

Self-massage is something we can all build into our daily lives. Ideally, give yourself an all-over massage with warm oil before showering in the morning. If you are suffering from stress, a soothing massage before bed is a must.

Massage not only makes you feel good, it stimulates and energizes the mind and body, slows the ageing process, softens superficial and deep tissues, nourishes the nervous system and improves the skin and complexion, as well as easing conditions such as arthritis, osteoporosis and sinusitis. Used daily, massage really can help you to cope better with everyday pressures by making you feel more relaxed, focused, energized and resilient.

Make sure you choose the base oil – and any aromatherapy essences you may want to add – to suit your constitutional type. Sesame oil is the best base oil for Vata; sunflower or coconut oil are cooling for Pitta. Corn oil is good for Kapha types or, alternatively, you can use a dry bristle body-brush or massage yourself with powdered chickpeas for a more stimulating effect.

When choosing aromatherapy essences, keep in mind that sweet, floral fragrances tend to balance Vata and Pitta, while spicy, pungent scents work best for Kapha dosha. Sandalwood, rose, lotus flower, frankincense, cinnamon and basil pacify Vata; sandalwood, rose, vetivert, lemon grass, lavender, lily, saffron and honeysuckle pacify Pitta; camphor, cinnamon, cloves, sage, thyme, cedar and frankincense pacify Kapha. Simply add ten drops to your chosen base oil.

Apply about 200–300ml of warm (not hot) oil all over the body, starting with the head and working downwards. Leave the oils on for 30 minutes before having a bath or shower. Remember to tailor your massage technique to suit your constitution, using gentle strokes for Vata and more vigorous ones for Kapha types.

If you don't have time for a full body massage, applying a little oil or ghee (clarified butter) to the top of the head and soles of the feet is surprisingly effective.

The five methods of internal cleansing

'Panchakarma' is one of the most powerful tools in Ayurveda's medicine chest. These five methods of internal cleansing purge the body of deep-seated toxins and restore the doshic balance. They are used to treat many serious, chronic and acute conditions including multiple sclerosis, asthma and stubborn skin complaints, as well as to promote good health by detoxifying the mind and body.

Caution

Panchakarma is a complex and lengthy process, which takes around five to six weeks to complete and must only be administered by a highly qualified and experienced Ayurvedic doctor.

Panchakarma works by drawing deep-rooted ama and aggravated doshas from the tissues of the body and returning them to the GI tract ready for elimination by one or more of the following five methods:

- Vamana (emesis or vomiting therapy) is used to treat conditions caused by excess Kapha dosha, such as bronchial asthma, sinusitis and skin problems like urticaria. It is best done in spring when Kapha tends to aggravate.

- Virechana (purgative therapy) is the best way to eliminate Pitta dosha from the small intestines, pancreas, spleen and liver and correct the body's metabolism. It is one of the most energizing treatments and a powerful cure for many deep-rooted conditions including stubborn skin diseases, digestive upsets, allergies, vascular and gynaecological problems. It is best given in late summer when Pitta is most intense.

- Basti (medicated enema) removes Vata from the colon and is often given after virechana or vamana to balance the system. The fact that most diseases are due to some degree of Vata aggravation, and that the quickest route for medicines to be absorbed is via the colon, makes basti a potent treatment. A combination of nourishing and purifying enemas are usually given to lubricate the colon and remove specific pathogens. Basti is used to treat degenerative conditions such as rheumatoid arthritis, Alzheimer's and Parkinson's disease as well chronic constipation and sciatica.

- Nasya (nasal therapy) treats diseases of the head and neck including migraine, sinusitis and allergic rhinitis. After a short localized massage, a medicated liquid or powder is dropped into each nostril.

- Raktamoksha (blood-letting) is used to treat conditions such as gout and blood disorders due to extreme Pitta aggravation. Blood-letting with leeches is used in many parts of the world today and is even making a comeback in Western medicine.

Before one or more of these powerful cleansing processes can be applied, the patient must be carefully prepared via a strict dietary regimen, the consumption of ama-digesting herbs, drinking, massaging the body with oily substances and using heat therapy such as steam baths and saunas. This process loosens deep-rooted ama from the tissues, and helps to return them to the GI tract, while lubricating and opening the channels of the body ready for purgation.

Fasting as an alternative to panchakarma

If you don't have the time or access to a panchakarma specialist, fasting is an extremely effective alternative. It is best done at the turn of each season as it helps your body adjust to changes in diet and the weather. It is very important, however, to pick a time when you can get plenty of rest as this is a powerful, often emotional process. It is also essential to match your fasting method to your constitutional type which you can identify using the dosha-finder questionnaire provided in the next chapter.

Fasting purges our bodies of the toxins and residues that mount up over years of eating foods that are high in fat and protein, as well as sharpening our mental faculties. It also helps to promote weight loss and reduces any swelling or water retention.

In Ayurvedic terms, it corrects any digestive problems and helps to restore our innate doshic balance while cleansing the vital organs and channels of the body – such as the veins and GI tract – thus ensuring that our tissues are properly nourished. In other words, fasting improves the overall function of our minds and bodies, providing tranquillity, strength, energy and vitality.

Be aware that as your body rids itself of unwanted toxins you may experience some side effects such as headaches, irritability, fatigue and sweating more than usual.

Caution

Fasting is an intense process. It should not be undertaken when the weather is very hot or cold, if you are feeling weak or unwell, if you are pregnant or breast-feeding or if you have very high levels of Vata in your system. If you suffer from an on-going medical condition or are taking any medication, consult your doctor before undertaking any fasting regimen.

Phase One: Preparing your body

For the first three days drink two teaspoons of ghee (see Chapter 6 for recipe) dissolved in a cup of hot water in the early morning on an empty stomach. If you are a Vata type add a pinch of rock salt to your ghee; if Kapha add a pinch of Trikatu (see Appendix 2 for suppliers). Pitta types should drink plain ghee. This internal oleation process loosens toxins lodged deep in the tissues.

Throughout the day eat only mung-bean soup and nothing else! You can have as much of it as you like, but only eat when you are really hungry and once your previous meal has been fully digested. As a general rule this means leaving three to four hours between each meal.

Mung-bean soup is highly nutritious and naturally detoxifying. It works by cleansing the liver, gall bladder and vascular system of any undigested toxins.

Recipe for mung-bean soup

You can use either whole green mung beans or the split yellow variety. Wash the beans thoroughly before soaking them overnight or for at least 2 hours. Heat some ghee in a pan, add a tsp of turmeric powder, 2 pinches of asafoetida and 2 bay leaves (all these ingredients are available in Asian food stores and most health-food shops). Add 1 part mung beans to 3 parts water, some freshly grated ginger root and simmer for 30 to 40 minutes, adding more water if necessary. In a separate pan, briefly sauté 1 tsp of cumin and coriander seeds with some finely chopped onion, until the onions are soft, and then add 2 to 3 cloves of chopped garlic at the end, sautéing them briefly. Add this mix to the beans once they are properly cooked and simmer for a few minutes. Season with rock salt to taste.

If you feel like having a break from eating mung, then a watery soup made from pumpkin, courgettes or green leafy vegetables can be substituted for one of your meals each day. Alternatively, you can add these vegetables to the mung-bean soup recipe for a bit of variety.

The fasting period

Throughout the preparation period (when only soup is consumed), the actual fasting period itself (when no food is eaten at all) and for at least five days afterwards, drink the fasting drink recipe recommended for your constitutional type throughout the day.

For the actual period of fasting, it is recommended that Vata types – who are typically low in stamina – fast for no more than one day; Pitta types can fast for one and a half days; while more robust Kapha types can fast for a maximum of two days if they feel strong enough. Time your fast so that it falls on a weekend when you can rest and relax.

Recipes for fasting drinks

Fasting drink for Pitta
3 cups of water
$\frac{1}{2}$ tsp cumin powder
$\frac{1}{2}$ tsp coriander powder
1 tsp rose water
3 cardamom seeds (ground in pestle and mortar)
$\frac{1}{2}$ tsp fennel-seed powder
1 pinch of asafoetida
4 fresh basil leaves
1 pinch of black pepper
1 tsp ginger juice (squeezed from a few slices of fresh ginger root)
Mix together in a pan, bring to the boil, simmer for 5 minutes, remove and cool for 20 minutes. Filter and keep warm in a thermos flask and drink regularly throughout the day.

Fasting drink for Vata
As above plus $\frac{1}{4}$ tsp ajwain powder and $\frac{1}{4}$ tsp dried ginger powder.

Fasting drink for Kapha
3 cups of water
2 tsp ginger juice
10 basil leaves (crushed and made into a juice)
1 pinch asafoetida
2 pinches black pepper
$\frac{1}{2}$ tsp cumin powder

Along with the fasting drink, make sure you drink at least two litres of pure water at room temperature or above every day. Never drink iced or cold water as it reduces your digestive fire. You can also drink plenty of herbal teas made from digestive spices such as fennel, cumin and coriander seeds, turmeric or dry ginger powder. Whenever you feel hungry, have some more herbal tea or fasting drink to encourage your body to digest more toxins, accumulated mucus and old, undigested food.

It is important that you get maximum rest on the days of your fast. Ideally you should be alone and somewhere peaceful. Explain what you are doing to your family and friends and ask them to give you the space to rest and relax. Prepare your home environment with soothing aromatherapy oils, sweet-smelling flowers and candles so you can relax in harmonious surroundings. Use this time for gentle contemplation, meditation, luxurious self-massages with warm sesame oil, taking long hot baths, listening to peaceful music, inspirational reading and taking gentle strolls in beautiful, natural surroundings to soothe your mind and soul.

Break your fast after the one to two days stipulated for your constitutional type with a small portion of manda (see recipe on page 44) without ghee. It is very important to finish your fast in this way so you do not overstretch your digestive fire, which has just been restored by the fasting process.

Post-fasting diet

Now your digestive fire has been rekindled, it is important to return to your normal diet gradually. Five days is the absolute minimum amount of time required before a wider variety of foods can be reintroduced.

During this time, follow the dietary regimen and recipes provided and remember to eat small portions *only* when you are hungry and your last meal has been fully digested.

- Day 1: manda without ghee
- Day 2: manda with ghee
- Day 3: peya with ghee
- Days 4 and 5: vilepi with ghee

This light diet helps to flush out any remaining toxins from the GI tract while readying your system to the point when it is able to cope with normal food again. If any other type of food is taken at this stage it will not be digested correctly which means new toxins will form, undoing all your good work!

Recipes for manda, peya and vilepi

These are three types of 'khichadi', a traditional Indian dish which is very easy to digest and highly nutritious.

- Manda: 1 part rice/mung beans/vegetables to 8 parts water
- Peya: 1 part rice/mungs beans/vegetables to 6 parts water
- Vilepi: I part rice/mung beans/vegetables to 4 parts water

Wash and soak the mung beans for at least 2 hours or overnight. Heat a tablespoon of ghee in a pan, add a teaspoon of cumin seeds, finely chopped onion, fresh ginger root and garlic and sauté until golden brown. Stir in 1 tsp turmeric powder, $\frac{1}{8}$ tsp asafoetida, some black pepper, bay leaves, $\frac{1}{2}$ tsp coriander powder and 1 tsp garam masala. Add $\frac{1}{2}$ cup rice, $\frac{1}{4}$ cup mung beans and $\frac{1}{4}$ cup chopped vegetables such as carrot, pumpkin, courgettes or asparagus. Now add the required amount of water and cook for 30 minutes. Serve with a little ghee and fresh coriander leaves. Manda should have a very watery consistency; peya is more soup-like; while vilepi is thicker still.

Your schedule for the fasting process

The following chart is a general guide, but remember that if you are a Vata type your actual fast will last for just one day, so the total fasting regimen will last for nine days; if you are Pitta you need to fast for one and a half days, so the total regimen will last for nine and a half days; if you are Kapha you can fast for a maximum of two days, so the total regimen will run for the full ten days indicated in this chart.

Day	Drink ghee	Mung bean soup	Fasting drink	Monodiet of kichadi
1	X	X	X	
2	X	X	X	
3	X	X	X	
4			X	
5			X	
6			X	X (break your fast with a small portion of manda without ghee)
7			X	X (manda + ghee)
8			X	X (peya + ghee)
9			X	X (vilepi + ghee)
10			X	X (vilepi + ghee)

When you have completed your fasting regimen and are ready to start eating normal foods again, take care to avoid those foods that are particularly hard to digest, such as meat and wheat products, for the first 14 days.

Useful herbal remedies

During a fast some people experience constipation. In case this occurs, have some Triphala tablets on hand and take them at night before bed with warm water. In Appendix 2 you will find a list of recommended suppliers.

Revitalizing your mind and body

'Rasayana' – or rejuvenation therapy – is the third and final step in the healing of any disease and is also used preventatively to build our natural immunity or 'ojas'. It is a powerful anti-ageing therapy that speeds up the process of cellular renewal, helping to promote longevity, fertility, a healthy state of mind and youthful complexion.

Certain types of food, herbal and mineral remedies, as well as wholesome mental and physical practices are considered to be rasayanas because of the revitalizing effect they have on the mind and body. Physical activities that are rejuvenating include therapeutic massage, linking with nature, rest and sleep, as well as eating naturally revitalizing foods such as rice, milk and ghee. Mental activities that are rejuvenating include positive methods of mind control, yoga, pranayama and meditation, as well as ethical conduct.

How rasayanas work

In conventional medical terms, the effect of rasayanas that are consumed is explained by the fact that these rejuvenating natural substances are able to penetrate deep into the cells of the body, halting the continuous process of bodily decay by nourishing our tissues at a microcellular level and speeding up cellular renewal. This explains why they are potent anti-ageing solutions.

Rasayanas also normalize our sensitivity to white blood cells, making them an effective treatment for allergic diseases – such as eczema, urticaria and allergic dermatitis – caused by the hypersensitivity of these cells to certain antigens rather than a breakdown in immunity.

Many rasayana substances – such as the fruit Amalaki (Emblica officinalis) – are also rich in antioxidants and adaptogenic in effect, so helping the body to adjust and fight disease. Amalaki actually has the highest concentration of vitamin C of any natural substance known to man, equivalent to the juice of 20 lemons! Ashwagandha (Withania somnifera) is another adaptogenic herb and natural rejuvenator. By speeding up cellular regeneration, it reduces the signs of ageing and acts as a powerful nervine tonic and aphrodisiac.

In Ayurvedic terms, rasayanas work by improving digestion so that our tissues are properly nourished and ojas, the essence of the seven tissues and our innate immunity factor, is produced in abundance. The diagram below helps to illustrate this process.

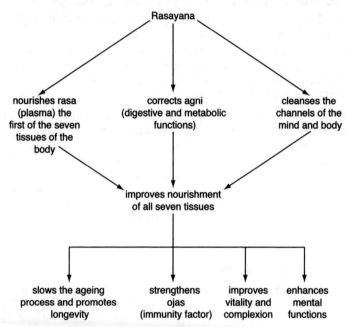

figure 2 How rasayanas work on the mind and body

Typically, rejuvenating substances are cold, heavy and sweet-tasting in nature. Organic milk and ghee are good examples of natural food rasayanas, while honey and onions are also said to have an immediate revitalizing effect on the tissues of the body. Common Ayurvedic remedies with a rejuvenating effect include

Shatavari (Asparagus racemosus), Ashwagandha, Guggulu (Commiphora mukul) and Triphala. You'll find more information on these remedies in Chapter 9.

Revitalizing acts include wholesome methods of mind control, such as when we use our powers of descrimination, courage, willpower and practise self-awareness. Consider how, when we do 'the right thing', we feel more contented. Ayurveda calls this state of mind 'Sattvic'; it is a state of being that is nourishing to our mind, body and soul.

Why we need rasayanas today

Taking a daily rasayana does not give you cast-iron protection. You may still fall sick but, if you do, your body now has the reserves to fight off an illness more quickly and without complications.

Five thousand years ago, the founders of Ayurveda noted that 'urbanites' became sick more often because of overcrowding and environmental pollution. In our urbanized world, mental and medicinal rasayanas are a natural way to stay healthy and happy.

In the next chapter you will find some simple rasayana formulations and practices you can use to promote good health.

part two

two

putting Ayurveda
into practice

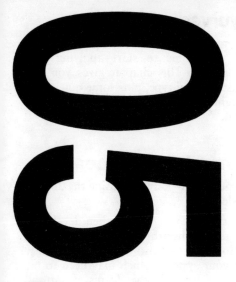

05

getting started

In this chapter you will learn:
- how to diagnose your mind–body type
- typical features of the key constitutions
- healthy living tips to suit your constitution
- simple ways to cleanse and fortify your digestion
- herbal remedies to boost your immunity
- healthy mental practices you can start to apply.

Building your Ayurvedic way of life

In Part One, we got to grips with the basic principles of Ayurvedic wisdom. Now it is time to start applying this knowledge to your everyday life. This chapter gives you the tools to diagnose your constitutional type, plus some quick and easy steps you can take – right now – to improve your digestion, immunity and state of mind.

Identifying your mind–body type

Let's begin by identifying your mind–body type using the dosha-finder questionnaire provided.

Knowing your mind–body type means you can then develop a diet and lifestyle routine that is healthy for your particular make-up. This same questionnaire can also be used to identify any current imbalances in your system, which may need to be treated with foods, herbs, exercise and other forms of natural therapy.

The dosha-finder works by assessing a series of physical, mental and biological traits according to the qualities and functions we know are controlled by one of the three doshas, Vata, Pitta and Kapha, and using these to determine your specific doshic balance.

Do be aware that this dosha finder is only a rough guide for your personal use. The subtleties of our mind and body are many, which is why an experienced Ayurvedic practitioner is really the best person to give a definitive diagnosis. This is a tool you can use now to establish the basics, however.

Before completing the questionnaire, keep in mind the following facts that have already been mentioned:

- We each have a unique combination of all three doshas, but usually one or more will predominate.
- It is this unique doshic balance that dictates our specific physical appearance, mental traits and personality, as well as our predisposition to certain diseases. This explains why no two people are exactly the same.
- Our constitutional type is created at the point of our conception and is unchanging. However, if one or more of the

doshas becomes aggravated this can lead to particular health problems, depending on which qualities are disturbed.

- For good health to be achieved, we must restore our natural doshic balance and then take action to preserve this equilibrium via an appropriate diet and lifestyle regimen tailored to suit our unique mind–body type.

Tips on making your diagnosis

It is a good idea to photocopy and then complete the dosha-finder questionnaire twice:

- The first time, use it to identify your natural constitutional type. This means you need to think about how your mind and body function naturally, rather than how they are at this point in time, when making your response. If you are usually a sound sleeper, for instance, but are currently having trouble sleeping, tick the box for being a sound sleeper as this is your natural state. Try to remember how you were as a child; were you naturally slim, for instance, but now suffer from weight gain? If so, then your natural build is slim but you are suffering from an imbalance of Kapha dosha.
- The second time you complete the dosha finder, think about how you are now and answer the questions accordingly. It could be that your bowel movements are usually regular but you have been constipated recently; tick the appropriate box.

If you feel that you fluctuate between two statements, for instance you gain and lose weight rapidly, tick the box for Vata, which is erratic by nature. If you think two characteristics apply to you equally, tick them both.

At the end of each round, count up the number of ticks awarded to each dosha. This will give you your mind–body type and identify any doshic imbalance.

It is important to answer all the questions as accurately and honestly as you can. Remember, there is no right or wrong constitutional type and only by gaining a truthful picture can you start to build a way of life that is healthy for you. It may help to ask a friend to complete the dosha finder on your behalf and then compare the results.

Your dosha-finder questionnaire

Feature	Vata	V	Pitta	P	Kapha	K
Height	Unusually tall or very short		Medium		Usually short but can be tall	
Body frame	Thin and bony with prominent joints		Moderate, athletic, good muscles		Large, well developed	
Weight	Low, find it hard to gain weight		Moderate		Heavy, gains weight easily	
Complexion	Dull or dusky, tans easily		Ruddy, freckly, burns easily		Lustrous, pale and smooth	
Skin texture	Rough, dry, thin		Warm and oily		Cold, oily, thick	
Eyes	Small, dry, nervous, often brown		Sharp, penetrating, green, blue or grey with yellowish sclera		Big, beautiful, loving, calm	
Hair	Dry, thin, curly		Fine and slightly oily, maybe red or light brown, prone to premature grey or balding		Thick, oily, wavy, lustrous	
Teeth	Crooked, poorly formed		Medium, soft tender gums which bleed easily		Large, straight, white	
Nose	Uneven, deviated septum		Long, pointed, red tip		Large but in proportion	
Nails	Rough, hard, brittle, split easily		Soft, pink, lustrous		Whitish, pale, smooth and polished	

Feature	Vata	V	Pitta	P	Kapha	K
Lips	Very thin, dry or chap easily		Medium, soft, pink		Thick, large, smooth and firm	
Chest	Narrow, small breasted (women)		Medium		Broad and muscular, big breasted (women)	
Belly	Thin, flat, sunken		Moderate		Big, pot-bellied	
Hips	Narrow		Moderate		Broad, heavy	
Joints	Stiff, prominent, crack easily		Loose, moderate, sprain easily		Firm, large, well lubricated	
Appetite	Erratic, eyes bigger than stomach!		Strong, excessive		Moderate but steady	
Circulation	Poor		Good		Moderate	
Menstruation	Irregular, scanty		Regular, prolonged		Regular, effortless, prone to water retention	
Sweating	Very little strong odour		Profuse		Slow to start but then sweats profusely	
Urine	Small but frequent amounts		Abundant, deep yellow, prone to burning sensation		Moderate and clear	
Stool	Hard, dry, dark, prone to constipation		Soft, loose, prone to diarrhoea		Regular, oily, heavy	
Digestive ability	Irregular, forms gas		Quick, causes burning		Prolonged, forms mucus	
Physical activity	Hyperactive		Moderate		Sedentary, slow and deliberate	

Feature	Vata	V	Pitta	P	Kapha	K
Mental activity	Always alert, easily distracted		Intense, efficient, perfectionist		Slow and considered	
Immunity	Low, variable strong		Moderately		Strong, rarely gets sick	
Stamina	Poor, easily exhausted		Moderate		Strong and steady	
Sex drive	Frequent desire, low stamina		Moderate desire, passionate		Variable, sometimes insatiable, good stamina	
Sensitivities	Cold, dry, windy weather		Heat and light sensitive		Cold, damp conditions	
Disease tendency	Pain, fatigue, nervous disorders		Fever and inflammation, ulcers and skin problems		Congestion, swelling, respiratory problems	
Speech	Fast and frequent		Direct, assertive, sharp		Slow melodious direct,	
Gait	Walk quickly		Purposeful pace		Slow, graceful unhurried	
Social	Insecure in new situations		Outgoing and assertive		Quiet but charismatic	
Temperament	Nervous, changeable		Highly motivated		Generally content	
Memory	Learn fast, forgets easily		Sharp, clear		Slow to learn but retentive	
Sleep	Poor, disturbed		Sound		Excessive, difficulty waking	
Dreams	Many, active, fearful		Moderate, passionate, fiery		Infrequent, calm, romantic	
Positive emotions	Adaptable		Courageous		Loving	

Feature	Vata	V	Pitta	P	Kapha	K
Negative emotions	Fearful		Angry		Depression and greed	
Faith	Variable		Strong, extremist		Consistent, deep and mellow	
Forgiveness	Forgive and forget easily		Hold grudges		Understanding, rarely get upset	
Financial	Spend impulsively on trifles		Spend moderately, enjoy luxuries		Generally frugal, but spend freely on food and entertainment	
Total	**Vata**		**Pitta**		**Kapha**	

Interpreting your results

Now count up the number of Vata, Pitta and Kapha answers. Normally one or two doshas will predominate to give you your prakriti when you complete the questionnaire the first time. The second time around, the results give an insight into the nature of any doshic imbalance you may be suffering from currently.

If one dosha clearly predominates consider yourself lucky; this is quite rare but makes it very easy to develop a way of life that keeps this in balance. Most of us, however, have 'dual' personalities, with a relatively equal split of two doshas – Vata-Kapha, for example – which are almost totally opposite in terms of their qualities and so harder to keep in balance.

In the latter case, depending on the circumstances at the time, one of the two predominant doshas will take control. For instance, if you are a Vata-Kapha type, in the cooler, dry, windy weather typical of autumn/fall, Vata will aggravate and become the dominant factor. At this time of year it is extremely important for people of this constitutional type to adopt a way of life that pacifies Vata dosha by favouring warm, nourishing foods, oily massages, low-impact exercise and soothing mental practices. In spring, Kapha is likely to take control, which means you will need to adopt a lighter diet, take more exercise and find ways to actively stimulate your mind.

This is why you need to stay alert and modify your routine in keeping with the rhythms of your body and nature. Remember to use your diary to track any particular triggers or patterns in your state of mind and body.

The typical imbalances today

The rapid pace of modern life, trend for convenience foods and thirst for commercial and financial success, means that most of the imbalances today are due to Pitta or Vata aggravations.

The increasing incidence of irritable bowel syndrome and anxiety, for example, are signs of aggravated Vata, while digestive problems, ulcers and hypertension (now one of the biggest killers worldwide) are Pitta-related conditions. There's a good chance, therefore, that any imbalance you have identified is due to one of these doshas.

These lifestyle influences also mean that, today, people with purely Kapha constitutions are extremely rare. We are living in a world that is dominated by Vata and Pitta qualities, thus the majority of us have a predominance of these doshas in our constitutional make-up. If your constitution analysis indicates a strongly Kapha influence or Kapha imbalance, the chances are that you actually have very high levels of ama (undigested toxins) in your system and a weakened digestive capacity. This is leading to Kapha-like symptoms – such as lethargy, a sluggish digestion, build-up of mucus and weight gain – rather than a predominantly Kapha constitution or excessive levels of Kapha dosha in your body. Following the fasting regimen given in Chapter 4 or the seven-day cleansing diet described in this chapter, will help to restore your digestive power and correct any imbalance.

More about your constitutional type

Now let's look at the typical features of the various constitutional types – be they Vata, Pitta, Kapha or a combination of these biological temperaments – and what we can do to keep them in balance.

Typical features of Vata types

We already know that the specific qualities of Vata dosha – being composed of air and ether – are cold, dry, light, rough, mobile, subtle, clear and astringent. As a result, people with a predominantly Vata constitution often suffer from dry skin and hair, cracked or split nails and cracking joints. Typically, they are highly prone to constipation or fluctuating bowel movements. They have a restless disposition – constantly on the move, walking and talking rapidly. The abundance of cold, dry qualities in their nature also makes them uncomfortable in cold, windy weather and means they crave warmth.

Physically they tend to be slightly built, underweight and have a relatively low level of immunity. Their appetite is variable and, while their sexual desire can be intense, they lack stamina.

People with a predominantly Vata constitution are quick thinking, creative and excellent communicators but they are also prone to nervous disorders such as stress, anxiety and insomnia. Professionally they are often artists, or work in the media or marketing industries.

Because of their active and restless nature, they are drawn to high-impact sports; however, more calming forms of exercise, such as yoga or pilates, are actually much better for their health.

The next table gives a snapshot of the principle qualities of Vata dosha and how these translate into particular mental and physical attributes.

Quality	Typical traits, mental and physical characteristics
Dry	Dry hair, skin and lips; prone to constipation, arthritis and brittle bones; sweat very little.
Light	Fragile 'bony' body frame with underdeveloped muscles; likely to be thin/underweight and lose weight easily; lack stamina; typically light sleepers (5–7 hours a night); prone to insomnia and vivid dreams.
Rough	Rough, cracked nails; cracking joints a common feature; may have coarse or curly hair.
Subtle	'Worriers' with a predisposition for anxiety-related problems such as fear, feelings of insecurity and isolation.
Cold	Suffer from poor circulation (cold nose, hands and feet); crave warmth and hate cold, dry, windy weather.

Mobile	Quick thinkers, talkers and movers; restless disposition; learn fast but forget easily; difficulty concentrating and completing tasks; weak willpower; love travelling/new adventures; fluctuating moods and appetite; drawn to high-impact exercise; powerful but erratic sex drive; spend impulsively, often on trifles.
Clear	Highly perceptive/sensitive, even clairvoyant; enthusiastic; creative; artistic; highly analytical; selfless and ready to help others.
Astringent	Prone to hiccoughs!

Healthy living tips to nourish Vata

If you've established that you are Vata predominant or have a Vata aggravation, the following actions can help you get it under control:

- Eat a warm, nourishing diet of predominantly sweet, sour and salty tasting foods such as unrefined wholegrains, pulses and dairy products, with a generous amount of oils and fats. One-pot wonders such as vegetable stews and soups are great for balancing Vata because they are packed full of nutrients and easy to digest.

- Have regular oily massages with warm sesame oil and sweet-smelling essential oils such as cinnamon, frankincense and lotus flower.

- Take hot baths and saunas to warm and release tension.

- Listen to soothing music and sounds to calm the mind.

- Practice yoga, pranayama (therapeutic breathing) and meditation to release tension, promote flexibility and pacify the mind.

- Establish a set routine of regular meals and bedtime.

- Sleep for around eight hours a night.

- Keep warm and avoid cold, drying conditions in general.

Typical features of Pitta types

The particular qualities of Pitta dosha are hot, sharp, slightly oily, quick, sour and pungent. Because of their 'fiery' nature, Pitta people are hot tempered and often intolerant or insensitive to others. Being extremely competitive, they excel in business and sport. Essentially, these people are high achievers with active, enquiring minds. Professionally they make good scientists, lawyers and business leaders.

One of the simplest ways to detect a Pitta personality is through their manner of speech. They tend to speak clearly, concisely and assertively. Another key indicator is their tendency to go grey or lose their hair prematurely!

Pitta people have strong, steady appetites for food and sex and tend to produce copious quantities of faeces, urine and sweat, all of which are often yellowish in colour due to the high levels of bile in their system.

Having more of the fire element in their make-up, these people are uncomfortable in hot weather, often suffering from heat-related complaints such as sunburn, rashes and pungent body odour.

Quality	Typical traits, mental and physical characteristics
Hot	Strong digestion; good circulation with above-average body temperature, so sweat easily and profusely; 'hot-headed' and irritable; quick-burning nature means they also go grey or bald prematurely; prone to fever, inflammation, hypertension, problems with liver and spleen.
Sharp (penetrating)	Incisive minds and intellect; good decision-makers; competitive, opinionated, judgemental; strong leadership qualities; sharp memory; can be intolerant and quick to criticize.
Light	Fair-skinned and light-sensitive; sunburn easily; skin likely to be freckled; sensitive skin and eyes so prone to acne, rashes and poor vision.
Liquid	Loose, yellowish stools; prone to diarrhoea; abundant urine and sweat.
Sour/pungent	Prone to acid indigestion and heartburn due to high acidic pH; strongly smelling sweat and other body odours.

Healthy living tips to cool Pitta

- Follow a diet that is rich in sweet, bitter and astringent tastes such as grains, fruit, asparagus and lettuce. Include some raw foods in your diet such as salads and leafy green vegetables.
- Use ghee instead of oil for cooking. It is cooling and rich in antioxidants, so helps to promote good eyesight and a healthy complexion.
- Avoid hot, spicy, sour foods and alcohol in excess.
- Seek cool and shady environments, especially in summer.
- Indulge in cooling and sweet-smelling perfumes such as sandalwood, lavender and rose.
- Exercise in moderation. Try not to be overly competitive!
- Wear 'cooling' colours, such as blue, green and white. Avoid vivid, hot tones which over-stimulate and irritate the mind.
- Massage with light oils such as almond, coconut and grapeseed.
- Try to be more patient and compassionate.

Typical features of Kapha types

The qualities of Kapha are cold, heavy, moist, oily, slow, smooth, firm, sticky and sweet. This means that physically Kapha people are well-built or stocky with a tendency to run to fat. Being well nourished, they have firm, smooth complexions, well-formed teeth and glossy, lustrous hair.

They have a slow but steady appetite and equally slow metabolism. Their languorous nature means they can be lazy and love to sleep! Sexually, their desire is slow to ignite but extremely passionate once aroused.

Psychologically, Kapha people are caring, devoted, loyal and steadfast, although their liking for creature comforts can make them possessive and even a little greedy. They are often slow to learn but will retain that knowledge. Their calm, steady, reliable disposition makes Kapha types excellent parents and providers. They are also great team players with compassion for others. Because of this, some of the most successful people have a largely Kapha constitution. It helps to explain their staying power and sense of purpose. You could describe them as the 'quiet achievers'.

However, their love of sweet, fatty foods and their sluggish metabolism makes them prone to lifestyle-related diseases such as diabetes and obesity. They are also susceptible to asthma, bronchitis and allergies.

Qualities	Typical traits, mental and physical characteristics
Cold	Cold, clammy skin; dislike cold, damp weather conditions; thrive in warm, arid conditions.
Moist	Supple, smooth skin; lustrous eyes and hair; prone to congestion in the chest, sinuses, throat and head, such as coughs and colds as well as water retention.
Heavy	Well-built, sturdy body frame; well-developed chest; prone to weight-gain and obesity.
Oily	Flexible, well-oiled joints; prone to mucus-related conditions such as lung congestion and sinusitis, cholesterolaemia and heart disease.
Slow	Sluggish metabolism; usually walk and talk slowly; learn slowly but retain knowledge for a lifetime; like to sleep excessively; can be lazy; avoid high-impact exercise despite plenty of stamina!
Firm	Steadfast, reliable disposition; well-nourished muscles and body tissues; robust complexion.
Sweet	Crave sweet tastes; susceptible to conditions such as type 2 diabetes, which can be acquired through an excess of sweet, fatty foods plus lack of exercise.

Healthy living tips for sluggish Kapha

- Follow a light diet of fresh, cooked, easily digestible foods – especially vegetables – with plenty of bitter, astringent and pungent tastes such as spinach and other green leafy vegetables, winter squash and asparagus cooked with warming digestive spices such as cardamom, ginger and cinnamon.
- Avoid eating too much mucus-producing food such as bread and pasta made from wheat, dairy products and beer.
- Honey is recommended. It has a drying effect as well as aiding digestion so helps to speed up a sluggish metabolism.
- The occasional fast can boost the metabolism and digest unprocessed foods and toxins stored in the GI tract.
- Take more high-impact exercise.
- Don't sleep for too long; seven hours a night is plenty! Above all, avoid the temptation to sleep during the day.

- Have dry massages which stimulate and energize.
- Make sure you keep warm and dry in cold, wet weather.

Dual constitutional types and their management

What if you have diagnosed yourself as a 'dual' constitutional type? As we have already noted, one of these two doshas will generally take control depending on the time of year and other external triggers such as pressures at home or at work.

In autumn/fall and early winter Vata usually aggravates; in the heat of summer Pitta is at its most intense; and in springtime Kapha typically takes control. If you are Vata-Pitta, therefore, you need to follow a diet and lifestyle to pacify Vata in autumn/winter and to pacify Pitta in the summer. If you are Pitta-Kapha, take steps to soothe Pitta in summer/autumn and balance Kapha in winter and spring. Stay vigilant and apply the appropriate healthy living tips to combat these doshic influences as and when they arise. Now let's look at the common features of dual personality types.

Features of Vata-Pitta types

Typically, these people suffer from poor circulation and crave heat but the Pitta element in their make-up means they are unable to tolerate extreme heat. They like to eat but have problems digesting large meals due to an erratic digestion.

When put under pressure, Vata-Pitta types fluctuate between feelings of fear and anger due to their in-built lack of self-esteem, and a strong urge to dominate and command. When these two emotions collide the result is a tendency to bully those weaker than themselves in an effort to assuage these two features of their personality.

When balanced, however, these people are both creative and highly focused. Their key weakness is a strong predisposition for unhealthy addictions, such as drugs and alcohol, a feature common to both Vata and Pitta doshas in isolation.

Their overriding requirement is stability at home and at work. These types should favour sweet-tasting foods and pursue Kapha-building activities, such as gentle types of exercise and wholesome mental practices, which help to stabilize their quick-witted but fiery natures.

Features of Pitta-Kapha types

This is an incredibly powerful combination. The world's most commercially successful people are often Pitta-Kapha types. It is a constitutional type that combines a powerful intellect and will to succeed with a calm, steady disposition and bucket loads of stamina and endurance.

Pitta-Kapha types are calm and resourceful in a crisis, mentally well-balanced and robust, with a healthy appetite for food, exercise and sex! Their principle weakness is that their innate strength can result in overconfidence, making them difficult people to live with. These people need to build their sense of intuition and consideration for others through candid self-reflection.

Bitter and astringent-tasting foods, which 'dry out' the overly oily qualities inherent in both Kapha and Pitta dosha, are required to balance these types mentally and physically.

Features of Vata-Kapha types

The overwhelming quality in these people is coldness, given that both Kapha and Vata are cold in nature. They need to eat plenty of warming foods with sour, salty and pungent tastes to counteract this and combat their susceptibility to problems such as constipation and respiratory complaints.

Physically they are usually tall and well-built. Personality-wise they are alternately open and friendly (a feature common of Vata types) and secretive and self-restrained (a Kapha trait). They are also highly sensitive, having a compassionate nature, coupled with the mood swings typical of Vata. It means they are sometimes difficult to understand, easily hurt and can lash out at others unexpectedly.

Now that we've learned to understand more about our innate mind–body type and how this translates into key physical and mental characteristics, we are ready to start applying Ayurvedic wisdom to our daily lives.

Seven-day diet to cleanse and fortify your digestion

In the previous few chapters we have established the importance of good digestion and the need to eliminate ama, the undigested food residues in our digestive tract which we all have and which has the power to impair the functions of our minds and bodies if left untreated, causing physical or mental disease.

If you do not have the time or opportunity to undertake a deep internal cleansing process such as one of those provided in Chapter 4, this simple diet is an effective way to start cleansing and fortifying your digestion.

As with all methods of detoxification, it is best to do this at the turn of the season – particularly the start of spring – as this is when the body needs all its energy to digest new varieties of food and adapt to changes in our environment.

1 For seven to ten days, follow a light diet of easily digestible foods such as freshly prepared vegetable juices, vegetable soups, steamed or stir-fried vegetables and boiled brown basmati rice. Vegetables to favour include pumpkin, courgette, spinach, asparagus, green beans, leeks, fennel, onions, carrots, parsnips, beetroot, celery, sweet potatoes, artichokes and mushrooms. Avoid potatoes, peppers, aubergine, cauliflower, broccoli and peas, or have them only occasionally.

2 These are the only foods you should eat. Eat only when you are hungry and avoid eating too much, snacking between meals or eating after 7p.m.

3 Season your food with natural digestives such as ghee, fresh ginger root, cumin, coriander, fennel seeds, turmeric, garlic, black pepper and cinnamon. These spices are all dry, light and hot in nature, so help to break down the heavy, cold, sticky substance that is ama and to stimulate your digestive fire.

4 Drink at least two litres of pure water, served at room temperature or above, every day. You can also drink herbal teas made from fresh ginger root, cumin or fennel seeds. Simply grate or crush these ingredients and steep them in a cup of hot water for five minutes before drinking.

5 Take one of Ayurveda's potent ama-digesting herbal remedies before each meal, such as Trikatu, Avipathika churna or Hingvastaka curna. This will help to speed up and intensify the cleansing process. In Chapter 9 you will find more information on the therapeutic effects of these formulations, and a list of suppliers of these and other authentic Ayurvedic remedies is provided in Appendix 2.

6 If your constitution analysis shows a strongly Vata prakriti or a Vata imbalance, take a teaspoon of castor oil with a pinch

of dry ginger powder in a glass of hot water at night. It's a powerful natural cleanser that will flush out and lubricate the colon, so helping to remove any dryness or blockages and restore the proper flow of Vata dosha through the channels of the body.

7 Make sure you get plenty of rest, and practise one of the methods of meditation given in Chapter 8 if possible. Meditating will help the cleansing process because it purifies our minds of negative thoughts and emotions, all of which have the power to build mental toxins and ama in the system.

Notice how, at the end of this process, your body feels lighter, your mind and senses more alert and energized. These are all signs that ama is being digested.

Once this process is complete, follow a diet to suit your particular constitutional type, as described in Chapter 6, and keep your digestion healthy by continuing to use natural digestives such as ghee, dry ginger powder and cumin seeds in your diet.

Note

Kapha types or people with cholesterol problems should use flaxseed oil, which is available from good health food stores, instead of ghee.

A daily dose of herbal rejuvenation

Once ama has been removed you can start taking a herbal rasayana. Be patient, as rasayanas take around 30 days to have an effect. You need to take them every day for prolonged periods of time to reap the rewards!

Chyawanaprash is a rejuvenating jam made from 40 herbs and fruits including Amalaki (Embilica officinalis). This general elixir has been used for thousands of years to promote immunity, strength and fertility. It builds haemoglobin and white blood cells, so increasing our resistance to infectious diseases and improving cellular regeneration. Take one to two teaspoons on an empty stomach every day with a cup of hot milk.

Single-herb rasayanas that are widely available include Ashwagandha (Withania somnifera), which is great for Vata types. This revitalizing herb is a powerful nervine tonic and is also extremely useful for treating allergies such as allergic rhinitis because it builds immunoglobins.

If your doshic analysis shows a Pitta predominance, try the cooling, bitter-sweet herb Shatavari (Asparagus racemosus). This is also a potent fertility-enhancing substance used for centuries to treat reproductive problems and symptoms of the menopause. Again, take one teaspoon in a cup of hot milk twice a day, morning and night.

Punarnava (Boerhavia diffusa) is good for Kapha types. As well as being restorative, it protects against conditions such as heart disease, oedema and water retention to which Kapha people are prone. Take one teaspoon twice a day in a cup of hot water.

Mental rasayanas

As we have already learned, rasayana therapies are designed to work on the mind as well as the body. The next step in creating a healthier way of life for yourself is to consciously build rejuvenating mental practices into your way of being. These practices will not only protect you from psychosomatic disorders such as stress, but will also build your sense of self-esteem. Good self-esteem is a critical factor in mental and physical wellbeing.

Self-observation, self-discipline, the application of knowledge and willpower are the key mental qualities to cultivate. Use them to catch and alter negative thoughts and to overcome unhealthy desires, such as overindulging in foods that you know to be contrary to your doshic harmony, for instance.

Here are some simple practices you can build into your life to get you started.

1 Make a list of all the negative thoughts, core beliefs and impressions you have accumulated over the years and start to replace them with more positive ones. For example, instead of telling yourself: 'I cannot change my life', tell yourself: 'I have the power to change'. Reciting simple mantras such as this to yourself daily really can shift negative perceptions and help you to realize your goals.

2 Use your imagination to visualize your aims and ambitions. If you can see the outcome you want to achieve, it is much more likely to become a reality. It's a technique that record-breaking athletes use to great effect.

3 Apply your intelligence and the knowledge you will gain from this book to create a healthier way of life according to your constitutional type, which includes a nutritious diet, regular

and appropriate levels of exercise, daily massage, sufficient rest and meditation.

4 Try to avoid being ruled by 'I'. Look deeper than your surface desires to establish what is appropriate behaviour at any point in time.

5 Find time to link with nature and do nourishing activities you enjoy, such as walking in the countryside, indulging in a long hot bath and listening to beautiful music. Note how this has a positive, healing effect on your state of mind.

6 Be with people who are positive and uplifting, especially in relationships.

7 Remember to apply the principles of samanya vishesha mentally, replacing fearful thoughts with safe, secure ones, angry thoughts with those of kindness and compassion.

8 Avoid excesses of all kinds.

9 Be realistic and consistent. Do a few practical things and stick at them!

06
how, when and what to eat

In this chapter you will learn:
- how to eat to suit your mind–body type
- the six tastes and their energetic effects
- foods to enjoy and foods to avoid
- healthy eating habits to cultivate.

Food as a form of medicine

A healthy diet – and how we eat it – is at the root of any healthy-living programme. In this chapter we will learn what foods are healthy for our specific constitutional type, as well as the healthy eating habits we need to cultivate to get the most from the food we eat.

Ayurveda sees food as a form of medicine. While slower to take effect than other medicines, its results are often more enduring and profound. Consumed wisely, food nourishes and heals our minds and bodies. Eating the 'wrong' foods and adopting poor eating habits, however, can kick start the disease process and are the root causes of many serious and life-threatening conditions today, including type 2 diabetes and obesity.

What makes Ayurveda's approach to diet unique is that, rather than promoting one diet to suit all, it recognizes us as individuals. It makes sense that slender, high-energy Vata types need more nourishing and sustaining foods than robust, slow-moving Kapha people; that Pitta people, who are prone to toxic disorders such as liver, skin and blood problems, need to eat more of the foods that are naturally cleansing and detoxifying. As a result, Ayurveda teaches us which foods we need to eat to balance our specific constitution or genetic blueprint and so avoid the diseases to which we are susceptible.

It is an approach that is now being embraced by Western nutritional experts. The 'new' science of Nutrigenomics, or the 'DNA Diet', says that by tailoring our diets to suit our specific genetic make-up, we can eat our way out of trouble, protecting ourselves from the illnesses to which we are genetically predisposed.

The foundation of a healthy, Ayurvedic diet is a balance of complex carbohydrates, such as rice and unrefined wholegrains, plus a variety of vegetables, pulses, nuts, seeds and seaweed to give us the proteins, minerals and vitamins essential for a healthy mind and body.

Following an Ayurvedic diet does not mean you have to be vegetarian, although many of its followers choose to avoid meat for ethical, health and karmic reasons. If you eat meat, however, you need to take steps to build your digestive strength by cooking with digestive herbs and spices, exercising regularly to speed up your metabolism and consuming it only in small portions once or twice a week rather than every day. This is because meat is much more complex to digest than most other foods and will putrefy in the gut if our digestion is not strong enough to cope with it or if we eat it too often.

Today, as well as adopting this basic diet and tailoring it to suit our constitutional type, we also need to take into account the denaturing (i.e. stripping of the natural) effect that modern farming and food processing methods have on the staple ingredients of the typical Western diet, such as dairy and wheat for instance. These processes can make foods which were originally wholesome, indigestible and toxic to our system.

Following an Ayurvedic diet in the 21st century therefore means taking the time to seek out foods in their natural, unpolluted state and preparing them in a healthy and wholesome way. Instead of buying everything you need from your local supermarket, check out the organic and bio-dynamically grown foods available from your local health food shop or farmers market, for example.

The power of taste

In Ayurveda the selection of both food substances and natural remedies is based on their energetic profiles, that is, their initial taste, thermal potency (either hot or cold) which occurs during the process of digestion and post-digestive impact.

Each of these three taste factors – known as rasa (initial taste), virya (thermal potency) and vipaka (post-digestive impact) – are inherent in a particular food substance and have a specific impact on the mind and body such as heating, cooling, drying, moistening, nourishing, lightening and detoxifying. This means they have a direct impact on our state of wellbeing because they have the power to preserve or disturb our doshic balance.

There are six tastes: sweet, sour, salty, bitter, pungent and astringent. Each has a specific effect on our doshic balance because of the basic elements and qualities it possesses.

- Dry ginger powder, for example, is pungent and sweet in taste, hot in potency and has a sweet post-digestive impact. As a result it reduces both Vata and Kapha dosha, which are predominantly cold in quality, builds Pitta and so improves our digestion as well as boosting circulation.

- Honey is sweet, astringent and hot in potency, so pacifies Vata and Kapha dosha. It has a drying effect on the body, making it useful for eliminating excess mucus and a powerful cardiotonic remedy.
- Onions are sweet and pungent, heavy and hot in potency, so reduce Vata and Kapha. The sweetness of their initial and post-digestive taste satisfies hunger and has an anabolic (building) effect on the body. As a result they are rejuvenating and promote tissue formation. Applied topically, onions can be used to relieve pain and inflammation due to their hot, sharp, penetrating qualities which pacify Vata dosha and promote good circulation, so delivering a soothing, analgesic effect.
- Garlic is hot and has five tastes: sweet, pungent, bitter, astringent and salty. This is why it has so many therapeutic benefits and is widely regarded as a 'cure all'. Like any medicine, however, it should be used wisely and with restraint. By balancing all three doshas, garlic rejuvenates the mind and body. Its hot quality digests mucus, making it an effective remedy for bronchitis, coughs and colds; it also improves the functions of the heart and promotes a vibrant complexion. In clinical studies, garlic has been found to lower bad (LDL) cholesterol and reduce blood clotting, making it a useful method of prevention for people at risk from heart attacks, strokes and atherosclerosis.
- Lemons are sour, bitter and cold. Their bitterness has a toning and detoxifying effect on the body because it prevents the build-up of Kapha. Their sour taste is appetizing and boosts digestive fire while balancing Vata. Having a sweet post-digestive taste, lemons also soothe Pitta dosha, unlike most other citrus fruits.

The next chart helps to illustrate how the six tastes work according to the five elements, their doshic impact, their thermal potency and inherent qualities, and gives some examples of food substances for each category of taste.

Taste	Five elements	Doshic impact	Thermal potency	Qualities	Therapuetic effect	Example
Sweet	Earth + water	VP↓K↑	Cold	Oily + heavy	Nourishing (anabolic); rejuvenating; tonic; laxative and diuretic	Rice, wheat (bread, pasta), lentils, pumpkin, milk, ghee (clarified butter), sugar
Sour	Earth + fire	V↓PK↑	Hot	Oily + heavy	Appetizer; digestive; carminative	Lemons, tomatoes, yoghurt, cheese, sour cream, vinegar and other fermented foods
Salty	Water + fire	V↓PK↑	Hot	Oily + heavy	Water-retaining so moisturizing; appetizer; digestive	Rock salt, seaweed, anchovies
Bitter	Air + ether	PK↓V↑	Cold	Dry + light	Detoxifying and drying; a digestive tonic in small doses	Turmeric, rhubarb, rocket, aloe vera, coffee, turmeric root
Pungent	Air + fire	K↓VP↑	Hot	Dry + light	Reducing (catabolic); digests mucus; improves circulation	Most spices, e.g. cumin, chilli, black pepper, onions, garlic, ginger
Astringent	Air + earth	PK↓V↑	Cold	Dry + light	Makes mouth pucker upon taste; absorbent; healing; purifying	Cranberries, pomegranates, unripe bananas, asparagus, brussels sprouts, chickpeas, okra, alfafa sprouts

A healthy diet includes all six tastes. Then you need to tailor it to your specific needs by emphasizing those tastes which balance your predominant dosha or the dosha which is likely to be aggravated at that point in time: Pitta in summer, Vata in autumn/fall and Kapha in winter and spring. The basic rule to remember and apply is that:

- sweet, sour and salty tastes balance Vata dosha
- sweet, bitter, astringent tastes balance Pitta dosha
- bitter, pungent, astringent tastes balance Kapha dosha.

Bitter is arguably the most therapeutic taste and is often lacking in the typical Western diet. In small quantities it balances all the other tastes, detoxifies the body and helps to ensure that all the channels of transportation within the body are working normally. In this way it promotes good health.

Bitter foods and condiments such as leafy green vegetables, mustard and black pepper are particularly useful for diabetics. Being opposite in qualities to the sweet, fatty foods which typically trigger this condition, they work by absorbing fat, cleansing the channels of the body and improving tissue formation.

The chart on pages 76–92 provides a useful guide to the tastes, potency and doshic effect of common dietary ingredients – including grains, fruits, vegetables, pulses, meat, cooking oils, nuts, seeds and spices – so you can begin to develop a diet suited to your specific needs.

Food Properties Chart

Food	taste (rasa)	Thermal potency (virya)	Post-digestive impact (vipaka)	Key qualities/ effects	Doshic impact		
Fruits							
Apple, ripe	Sweet, sour, astringent	Cooling	Sweet	Rough, light, dry	V↑	P↓	K↓
Apple, unripe	Astringent, sour	Cooling	Pungent	Rough, light, dry	V↑	P↓	K↓
Avocado	Sweet, astringent	Cooling	Sweet	Oily, heavy, soft	V↓	P↓	K↑
Apricots	Sweet, astringent	Heating	Sweet	Liquid, heavy	V↓	P↑	K↓
Berries, most sour	Sour	Heating	Pungent	Sharp, light	V↓	P↑	K↓
Berries, most sweet	Sweet	Cooling	Sweet	Oily, liquid	V↓	P↓	K↓
Banana, unripe/green	Astringent, sweet	Cooling	Sour	Heavy	V↓	P↓↑	K↓↑
Banana, ripe	Sweet, sour	Cooling	Sour	Smooth, heavy	V↓	P↑	K↑
Cantaloupe melon	Sweet	Heating	Sweet	Heavy, moist, builds ojas	V↓	P↓	K↑
Cherries (ripe)	Sweet	Cooling	Sweet	Light, liquid	V↓	P↓	K↓
Coconut	Sweet	Cooling	Sweet	Oily, hard	V↓	P↓	K↑
Cranberries	Astringent, sour	Heating	Pungent	Light, dry, sharp	V↑	P↑	K↓
Dates	Sweet	Cooling	Sweet	Heavy, energizing	V↓	P↓	K↑

	Taste	Energy	Post-digestive	Qualities	V	P	K
Figs (fresh)	Sweet	Cooling	Sweet	Heavy, energizing, rejuvenating	V↓	P↓	K↑
Grapes, green	Sour, sweet	Heating	Sweet	Liquid, strengthening	V↓	P↑	K↑
Grapes, red/purple/black	Sweet, sour, astringent	Cooling	Sweet	Light, energizing	V↓	P↓	K↑↓
Grapefruit	Sour	Heating	Sour	Acidic, hydrophilic	V↓	P↑	K↑
Kiwi	Sweet, sour, astringent	Cooling	Sweet	Light, moist	V↓	P↑	K↑↓
Lemon	Sour	Cooling	Sweet	Moist, detoxifying, appetizing	V↓	P↑	K↑
Lime	Sour	Cooling	Sweet	Light, refreshing, digestive	V↓	P↑↓	K↑
Mango, green	Sour, astringent	Cooling	Pungent	Heavy, hard	V↓↑	P↑	K↑↓
Mango, ripe	Sweet	Heating	Sweet	Energizing	V↓	P↓↑	K↑↓
Melons	Sweet	Cooling	Sweet	Heavy, moist	V↓	P↓	K↑
Oranges	Sweet, sour	Heating	Pungent	Moist, heavy	V↓	P↓↑	K↑↓
Papaya	Sweet, sour	Heating	Sweet	Heavy, oily	V↓	P↑	K↑↓
Peaches	Sour, sweet, astringent	Heating	Sweet	Heavy, liquid	V↓	P↑	K↑↓
Pears	Sweet, astringent	Cooling	Pungent	Dry, rough, heavy	V↓	P↓	K↓
Persimmon	Astringent, sour	Heating	Pungent	Light, dry, sharp	V↑	P↑	K↓

Food	taste (rasa)	Thermal potency (virya)	Post-digestive impact (vipaka)	Key qualities/effects	Doshic impact		
Pineapple	Sweet, sour	Heating	Sweet	Heavy, sharp	V↓	P↑	K↓↑
Plums	Sweet, sour, astringent	Heating	Sweet	Heavy, liquid	V↓	P↑	K↓
Pomegranate	Sweet, bitter, astringent	Cooling	Sweet	Smooth, oily	V↑	P↓	K↓
Prunes, soaked	Sweet	Cooling	Sweet	Soothing, laxative	V↓	P↓	K↓
Raisins, soaked	Sweet, sour	Cooling	Sweet	Soothing, laxative	V↓	P↓	K↑
Raisins, unsoaked	Sour	Cooling	Sweet	Light	V↓	P↓	K↑
Raspberries	Sweet, sour, astringent	Cooling	Pungent	Diuretic	V↑	P↓↑	K↓
Rhubarb	Sweet, sour	Heating	Sweet	Laxative, heavy	V↓	P↑	K↑
Strawberries	Sour, sweet, astringent	Cooling	Pungent	Laxative	V↑	P↓↑	K↓↑
Tamarind	Sour	Heating	Sour	Heating	V↓	P↑	K↑
Watermelon	Sweet	Cooling	Sweet	Heavy	V↑	P↓	K↑
Vegetables							
Artichoke, globe	Sweet, astringent	Heating	Sweet	Light, moist, diuretic	V↑	P↓	K↓
Artichoke, Jerusalem	Astringent, bitter	Cooling	Pungent	Light, dry, rough	V↑	P↓	K↓

Asparagus	Astringent, sweet, bitter	Cooling	Sweet	Soothing, good for all constitutional types	V↓	P↓	K↓
Aubergine (eggplant)	Bitter, astringent	Cooling	Pungent	Light, oily	V↓	P↑	K↓
Beetroot	Sweet	Heating	Sweet	Heavy	V↓	P↑	K↑
Beet greens	Astringent, sweet	Heating	Pungent	Light	V↓	P↑	K↓
Bitter melon	Bitter	Cooling	Pungent	Diuretic, regulates blood sugar	V↑	P↓	K↓
Broccoli	Pungent, astringent	Cooling	Pungent	Dry, rough	V↑	P↓	K↓
Brussels sprouts	Pungent, astringent	Heating	Pungent	Light, diuretic	V↑	P↓	K↓
Burdock root	Bitter, pungent, stringent	Heating	Pungent	Light, sharp, diuretic	V↑	P↓	K↓
Cabbage	Bitter, astringent	Cooling	Pungent	Heavy, dry, rough	V↑	P↓	K↓
Carrot, raw	Bitter, sweet, astringent	Cooling	Pungent	Hard, rough, heavy	V↑	P↑	K↓
Carrot, cooked	Sweet	Heating	Pungent	Light, soft	V↓	P↓↑	K↓
Cauliflower	Bitter, astringent	Cooling	Pungent	Dry, rough	V↑	P↓	K↓

Food	taste (rasa)	Thermal potency (virya)	Post-digestive impact (vipaka)	Key qualities/ effects	Doshic impact		
Celery	Salty	Cooling	Pungent	Dry, rough, light	V↓	P↓	K↓
Coriander leaf (cilantro)	Astringent, bitter, sweet	Cooling	Sweet	Light, oily, smooth	V↓	P↓	K↓
Corn, fresh	Astringent, sweet	Heating	Pungent	Light, dry, rough	V↑	P↑	K↓
Courgettes (zucchini)	Astringent	Cooling	Pungent	Heavy, liquid	V↓	P↓	K↑
Cucumber	Sweet, bitter, astringent	Cooling	Sweet	Liquid, soft	V↓	P↓	K↓↑
Dandelion greens	Bitter	Heating	Pungent	Light, diuretic	V↑	P↓	K↓
Fennel, fresh	Sweet, sour	Heating	Sweet	light, oily, sharp, laxative, diuretic	V↓	P↓	K↓
Garlic	Sweet, sour, bitter, pungent, astringent	Heating	Pungent	Oily, heavy, smooth, nourishing	V↓	P↑	K↓
Green beans	Sweet, astringent	Cooling	Pungent	Light	V↑	P↓	K↓
Kale	Bitter, astringent	Cooling	Sweet	Dry, rough	V↑	P↓	K↓
Kohlrabi	Astringent, pungent	Heating	Pungent	Sharp, light, diuretic	V↑	P↑	K↓

Leeks, cooked	Pungent, sweet	Heating	Sweet	Stimulant	V↓	P↓	K↓
Lettuce	Astringent	Cooling	Pungent	Light, liquid, rough	V↑	P↓	K↓
Mushrooms	Sweet, astringent	Cooling	Pungent	Light, dry	V↑	P↓	K↓
Mustard greens	Pungent	Heating	Pungent	Sharp, oily	V↓	P↑	K↓
Okra	Sweet, astringent	Cooling	Sweet	Soft, diuretic	V↓	P↓	K↓
Olives (black)	Sweet	Heating	Sweet	Heavy, oily	V↓	P↑	K↑
Onion, cooked	Sweet, Pungent	Heating	Sweet	Heavy, sharp, oily, digestive, carminative	V↓	P↑↑	K↓
Onion, raw	Pungent	Heating	Pungent	Heavy, appetizing	V↑	P↑	K↓
Parsnip	Sweet, astringent	Cooling	Sweet	Heavy, oily	V↓	P↓	K↑
Peas	Sweet, astringent	Cooling	Pungent	Hard, slow, heavy	V↑	P↓	K↓
Peppers (Bell)	Sweet, Astringent	Heating	Pungent	Dry, light,	V↑	P↓↑	K↓
Potato, sweet	Sweet	Cooling	Sweet	Soft, heavy	V↓	P↓	K↑
Potato, white	Astringent	Cooling	Sweet	Dry, light, rough	V↑	P↓	K↓
Pumpkin	Sweet	Heating	Sweet	Heavy	V↓	P↓	K↑
Radish	Pungent	Heating	Pungent	Hard, liquid, rough	V↑	P↑	K↓

Food	taste (rasa)	Thermal potency (virya)	Post-digestive impact (vipaka)	Key qualities/ effects	Doshic impact		
Rutabaga	Bitter, sweet	Cooling	Sweet	Heavy, oily	V↓	P↓	K↓↑
Spinach, raw	Bitter, astringent	Cooling	Pungent	Dry, light, rough	V↓	P↓	K↓
Spinach, cooked	Astringent, bitter, sour	Heating	Sweet	Heavy, laxative	V↓	P↑	K↓
Sprouts	Astringent	Cooling	Pungent	Light, moist	V↑	P↓	K↓
Squash, winter	Astringent, sweet	Heating	Pungent	Dry, sharp, heavy	V↑	P↓	K↓
Squash, summer	Sweet, astringent	Cooling	Pungent	Light, liquid	V↓	P↓	K↑
Tomato	Sour, Sweet	Heating	Sour	Disturbs all three doshas	V↓	P↑	K↑
Turnips	Pungent, astringent	Heating	Pungent	Rough, dry	V↑	P↑	K↓
Sweeteners							
Barley malt	Sweet	Cooling	Sweet	Oily, liquid	V↓	P↓	K↑
Date sugar	Sweet	Cooling	Sweet	Heavy, oily, energizing	V↓	P↓	K↑
Fructose	Sweet	Cooling	Sweet	Oily, liquid	V↓	P↓	K↑
Honey	Sweet, astringent	Heating	Sweet	Dry, light, scrapes clean	V↓	P↑	K↑
Jaggary	Sweet	Heating	Sweet	Heavy, nourishing	V↓	P↑	K↑

	Taste	Energy	Post-digestive	Qualities	V	P	K
Maple syrup	Sweet	Cooling	Sweet	Dry, light, scrapes clean	V↓	P↓	K↓
Molasses	Sweet	Heating	Sweet	Heavy, promotes bleeding	V↓	P↑	K↑
Rice syrup	Sweet	Cooling	Sweet	Oily, liquid	V↓	P↓	K↓
Sugar, white	Sweet	Cooling	Sweet	Heavy, oily, energizing	V↓	P↓	K↑
Grains							
Amaranth	Sweet, astringent	Cooling	Pungent	Light	V↓	P↓	K↓
Barley	Sweet	Cooling	Sweet	Light, diuretic	V↑	P↓	K↓
Buckwheat	Astringent, sweet, pungent	Heating	Sweet	Heavy	V↑↓	P↑	K↓
Corn	Sweet	Heating	Sweet	Dry, light	V↑	P↓	K↓
Durum wheat Flour (pasta)	Sweet, astringent	Cooling	Sweet	Heavy	V↓	P↓	K↑
Millet	Sweet	Heating	Sweet	Dry, light	V↑	P↓	K↓
Oat bran	Astringent, sweet	Cooling	Sweet	Rough, dry, light	V↑	P↓	K↓
Oats, dry	Sweet	Cooling	Sweet	Dry, rough	V↑	P↓	K↓
Oats, cooked	Sweet	Cooling	Sweet	Heavy	V↓	P↓	K↑
Quinoa	Sweet, astringent	Cooling	Sweet	Grounding	V↓	P↓	K↑↓
Rice, basmati	Sweet	Cooling	Sweet	Light, soft	V↓	P↓	K↓
Rice, brown	Sweet	Heating	Sweet	Heavy	V↓	P↑	K↑

Food	taste (rasa)	Thermal potency (virya)	Post-digestive impact (vipaka)	Key qualities/effects	Doshic impact		
Rice cakes	Astringent, sweet	Cooling	Sweet	Dry, light	V↑	P↓	K↓
Rice, white	Sweet	Cooling	Sweet	Holds water, soft	V↓	P↓	K↑
Rye	Bitter, astringent	Heating	Pungent	Dry, light	V↑	P↑	K↓
Sago	Astringent, sweet	Cooling	Sweet	Dry, light	V↑	P↓	K↓
Spelt	Pungent, astringent	Heating	Pungent	Light, dry	V↑	P↑	K↓
Tapioca	Astringent, sweet	Cooling	Sweet	Drying, Light	V↑	P↓	K↓
Wheat	Sweet	Cooling	Sweet	Heavy, oily	V↓	P↓	K↑
Pulses							
Aduki	Sweet, astringent	Cooling	Pungent	Hard, dry, heavy	V↑	P↓	K↓
Black-eyed peas	Sweet, astringent	Cooling	Pungent	Hard, heavy	V↑	P↓	K↓
Chickpeas	Sweet, bitter	Cooling	Pungent	Dry, rough, heavy	V↑	P↓	K↓↑
Kidney beans	Bitter	Heating	Pungent	Hard, rough, heavy	V↓	P↑	K↓

					V	P	K
Lentil, brown	Sweet, astringent	Heating	Pungent	Rough, heavy	V↑	P↓↑	K↓
Lentil, red	Sweet, Astringent	Cooling	Sweet	Light, soft	V↓	P↑	K↓
Miso	Astringent, sour	Heating	Pungent	Fermented	V↓	P↑	K↓
Mung beans	Sweet, astringent	Cooling	Sweet	Light, dry	V↓	P↓	K↓↑
Navy beans	Sweet, astringent	Heating	Pungent	Dry, rough	V↑	P↓	K↓
Pinto beans	Astringent	Cooling	Pungent	Hard to digest	V↑	P↓	K↓
Soya beans	Astringent, sweet	Cooling	Pungent	Oily, heavy	V↑	P↓	K↑
Soya cheese	Astringent, sour	Heating	Pungent	Heavy	V↓	P↑	K↑
Soya sauce	Astringent, sour	Heating	Pungent	Fermented	V↑	P↑	K↑
Tempeh	Astringent	Heating	Pungent	Light	V↑	P↓	K↓
Tofu	Sweet, astringent	Cooling	Pungent	Heavy, oily	V↓↑	P↑	K↓↑
Tur dal	Sweet, astringent	Heating	Pungent	Light, dry	V↓	P↑	K↑
Urad dal	Sweet	Heating	Sweet	Heavy, soft, oily	V↓	P↑	K↑
White beans	Astringent	Cooling	Pungent	Hard to digest	V↑	P↓	K↑

Food	taste (rasa)	Thermal potency (virya)	Post-digestive impact (vipaka)	Key qualities/effects	Doshic impact		
Dairy							
Butter	Sweet	Cooling	Pungent	Light, binds the stool	V↓	P↓	K↑
Buttermilk	Sweet, sour, astringent	Cooling	Sweet	Heavy, oily, binding	V↓	P↓↑	K↑
Cheese, hard	Sour	Cooing	Sour	Heavy, oily, mucus-producing	V↓	P↑	K↑
Cheese, soft	Sour	Cooling	Sour	Heavy, oily	V↓	P↑	K↑
Cottage cheese	Sour, salty	Heating	Pungent	Lighter, less heating	V↓	P↑	K↓
Cow's milk	Sweet	Cooling	Sweet	Heavy, mucus-producing	V↓	P↓	K↑
Ghee	Sweet	Cooling	Sweet	Oily, heavy, minute, kindles agni (digestive fire)	V↓	P↓	K↓↑
Goat's milk	Sweet	Cooling	Pungent	Light, nourishing	V↓	P↓	K↓
Ice cream	Sweet	Cooling	Sweet	Heavy, mucus-producing	V↑	P↓	K↑
Sour cream	Sour	Heating	Pungent	Heavy, oily	V↓	P↑	K↑
Yoghurt: freshly made	Sweet, sour	Cooling	Sweet	Mucus-producing	V↓	P↓	K↑
Yoghurt: old/store bought	Sour	Heating	Pungent	Mucus-producing	V↓	P↑	K↑
Animal foods							
Beef	Sweet	Heating	Sweet	Heavy	V↓	P↑	K↑

					V	P	K
Chicken, white meat	Astringent, sweet	Heating	Sweet	Light, oily	V↑	P↓	K↓
Chicken, dark meat	Sweet	Heating	Sweet	Heavy	V↓	P↑	K↑
Duck	Sweet, pungent	Heating	Sweet	Heating, heavy	V↓	P↑	K↑
Eggs	Sweet	Heating	Sweet	Oily, heavy	V↓	P↑	K↓↑
Eggs, yolk	Sweet	Heating	Sweet	Cholesterol increasing	V↓	P↑	K↑
Eggs, white	Sweet	Heating	Sweet		V↓	P↓	K↓
Fish, freshwater	Sweet, astringent	Heating	Sweet	Light, oily, soft	V↓	P↓↑	K↓↑
Fish, salmon	Sweet	Heating	Sweet	Oily	V↓	P↑	K↑
Fish, sea	Salty	Heating	Sweet		V↓	P↑	K↑
Fish, tuna	Sweet, salty, astringent	Heating	Pungent	Heating	V↓	P↑	K↑
Lamb and mutton	Sweet	Heating	Sweet	Oily, heavy	V↓	P↑	K↑
Pork	Sweet	Heating	Sweet	Oily, heavy	V↑	P↑	K↑
Rabbit	Sweet	Cooling	Pungent	Dry, rough	V↑	P↓	K↓
Shrimp	Sweet	Heating	Pungent	Light, oily	V↓	P↑↓	K↓
Turkey, white meat	Sweet, astringent	Cooling	Pungent		V↑	P↓	K↓
Turkey, dark meat	Sweet, astringent	Cooling	Pungent		V↑	P↑	K↑

Food	taste (rasa)	Thermal potency (virya)	Post-digestive impact (vipaka)	Key qualities/ effects	Doshic impact		
Venison	Astringent	Cooling	Pungent	Light, dry, rough	V↑	P↓	K↓
Nuts (soaked or ground)							
Almond (without skin)	Sweet, slightly bitter	Heating	Sweet	Oily, heavy, energizing	V↓	P↑	K↑
Almond (soaked peeled)	Sweet	Cooling	Sweet	Oily, heavy, energizing	V↓	P↓	K↑
Brazil	Astringent, sweet	Heating	Sweet	Oily	V↓	P↑	K↑
Cashew	Sweet	Heating	Sweet	Oily, heavy, energizing	V↓	P↑	K↑
Coconut	Sweet	Cooling	Sweet	Mucus-promoting	V↓	P↓	K↑
Hazelnut	Astringent, Sweet	Heating	Sweet	Energizing	V↓	P↑	K↑
Macadamia	Astringent, Sweet	Heating	Sweet	Energizing	V↓	P↑	K↑
Peanut	Sweet, astringent	Heating	Sweet	Oily, heavy, depleteing due to intense heat	V↓	P↑	K↑
Pecan	Astringent, sweet	Heating	Sweet	Oily, heavy	V↓	P↑	K↑
Pine nut	Astringent, sweet	Heating	Sweet	Very energizing	V↓	P↑	K↑

Pistachio	Sweet	Heating	Sweet	Oily, energizing	V↓	P↑	K↑
Walnut	Sweet	Heating	Sweet	Oily, heavy, energizing	V↓	P↑	K↑
Seeds							
Popcorn	Astringent, sweet	Cooling	Pungent	Dry, light, rough	V↑	P↓	K↓
Psyllium	Astringent	Cooling	Pungent	Dry, light, rough but still laxative in effect	V↑	P↓	K↓
Pumpkin	Sweet	Heating	Pungent	Oily, heavy, hard	V↓	P↓↑	K↓
Safflower	Sweet, astringent	Cooling	Sweet	Oily, light, soft	V↓	P↓	K↓
Sesame	Sweet, Bitter, astringent	Heating	Pungent	Oily, heavy, smooth	V↓	P↑	K↑
Sunflower	Sweet, astringent	Cooling	Sweet	Oily, light, soft	V↓	P↓	K↓
Oils (Kapha should use oils in very small amounts)							
Almond	Sweet	Heating	Sweet	Heavy	V↓	P↑	K↑
Avocado	Sweet	Cooling	Sweet	Oily, sweet	V↓	P↓	K↑
Castor oil	Sweet, Bitter	Heating	Sweet	Heavy, purgative	V↓	P↓	K↑
Coconut	Sweet	Cooling	Sweet	Unctuous, heavy	V↓	P↓	K↑
Corn	Sweet, astringent	Heating	Pungent	Dry, rough,	V↑	P↑	K↓
Canola	Astringent	Cooling	Pungent	Dry, rough, light	V↑	P↓	K↓
Mustard	Pungent	Heating	Pungent	Sharp, strong-smelling	V↓	P↑	K↓

Food	taste (rasa)	Thermal potency (virya)	Post-digestive impact (vipaka)	Key qualities/ effects	Doshic impact		
Olive	Sweet	Cooling	Sweet	Heavy, causes cellulite	V↓	P↓	K↑
Peanut	Sweet	Heating	Sweet	Strengthening	V↓	P↑	K↑
Safflower	Sweet, astringent	Heating	Pungent	Light, sharp, oily	V↓	P↑	K↑
Sesame	Sweet, astringent	Heating	Sweet	Penetrating, oily	V↓	P↑	K↑
Sunflower	Sweet, astringent	Cooling	Sweet	Soothing, lubricating	V↓	P↓	K↓
Herbs and spices							
Ajwain	Pungent	Heating	Pungent	Sharp, light, digestive	V↓	P↑	K↓
Allspice	Pungent	Heating	Pungent	Increases agni (digestive fire), liquefies Kapha	V↓	P↑	K↓
Anise	Pungent	Heating	Pungent	Light, detoxifying	V↓	P↑	K↓
Asafoetida (Hingu)	Pungent	Heating	Pungent	Dry, sharp, digestive	V↓	P↑↓	K↓
Basil	Sweet, pungent, astringent	Heating	Pungent	Diaphoretic	V↓	P↑	K↓
Bay leaf	Sweet, pungent, astringent	Heating	Pungent	Dilates channels of the body	V↓	P↑	K↓
Black pepper	Pungent	Heating	Pungent	Dry, sharp, digestive	V↓	P↑	K↓

	Taste	Heating/Cooling	Post-digestive	Qualities	V	P	K
Caraway	Sweet, astringent	Cooling	Pungent	Stimulates agni (digestive fire)	V↓	P↑	K↓
Cardamom	Sweet, pungent	Heating	Sweet	Light, oily, digestive	V↓	P↑↓	K↓
Cayenne	Pungent	Heating	Pungent	Hot, dry	V↓	P↑	K↓
Chillies	Pungent	Heating	Pungent	Sharp, dry	V↓	P↑	K↓
Cinnamon	Sweet, pungent	Heating	Pungent	Dry, light, oily	V↓	P↑↓	K↓
Clove	Pungent	Heating	Sweet	Light, oily	V↓	P↑↓	K↓
Coriander seeds	Astringent, bitter, sweet	Slightly heating	Sweet	Light, oily, smooth	V↓	P↑↓	K↓
Cumin	Pungent, bitter	Cooling	Pungent	Light, dry, digestive aid	V↓	P↓	K↓
Dill	Bitter, astringent	Heating	Pungent	Light, antispasmodic	V↓	P↑↓	K↓
Fennel	Sweet, pungent, bitter	Heating	Sweet	Light, oily, laxative	V↓	P↓	K↓
Fenugreek	Pungent, bitter	Heating	Pungent	Kindles agni (digestive fire)	V↓	P↑	K↓
Garlic	All tastes except salty	Heating	Pungent	Oily, heavy, smooth, nourishing	V↓	P↑	K↓
Ginger, dry powder	Pungent	Heating	Sweet	Light, oily, digestive	V↓	P↑	K↓
Ginger, fresh	Pungent	Heating	Sweet	Dry, heavy, ama digesting	V↓	P↑↓	K↓
Horseradish	Pungent, astringent	Heating	Pungent	Stimulates agni (digestive fire)	V↑↓	P↑	K↓
Mace	Pungent, astringent, sour	Heating	Pungent	Stimulates agni (digestive fire)	V↓	P↑	K↓

Food	taste (rasa)	Thermal potency (virya)	Post-digestive impact (vipaka)	Key qualities/ effects	Doshic impact
Marjoram	Pungent, astringent	Heating	Pungent	Stimulates agni (digestive fire)	V↓ P↑ K↓
Mint	Sweet	Cooling	Pungent	Calms Pitta	V↓ P↓ K↓
Mustard	Pungent	Heating	Pungent	Sharp, oily, light	V↓ P↑ K↓
Nutmeg	Sweet, astringent, pungent	Heating	Pungent	Stimulates agni (digestive fire)	V↓ P↑ K↓↑
Oregano	Astringent, pungent	Heating	Pungent	Digestive aid	V↓ P↑ K↓
Paprika	Pungent	Heating	Pungent	Stimulates agni	V↓ P↑ K↓
Parsley	Astringent pungent	Heating	Pungent	Stimulant, diuretic	V↓ P↑↓ K↓
Rosemary	Astringent, sweet	Heating	Pungent	Stimulant	V↓ P↑ K↓
Rock salt	Salty	Heating	Sweet	Absorbs moisture	V↓ P↑ K↑
Sea Salt	Salty	Heating	Pungent	Heavy, Hydrophilic	V↓ P↑ K↑
Saffron	Sweet, astringent, bitter	Heating	Sweet	Dry, light, aphrodisiac	V↓ P↓ K↓
Tarragon	Sweet	Cooling	Sweet		V↓ P↓ K↑
Turmeric	Bitter, pungent	Heating	Pungent	Dry, light, digestive aid	V↓ P↓ K↓

Eating to suit your mind–body type

Your constitutional type predetermines how much impact a particular taste has on your mind and body. Keep in mind that:

- if you are Kapha predominant you need to limit the amount of heavy, mucus-producing foods you eat – such as dairy products, wheat, refined sugar – and increase the quantity of drying substances, which are typically bitter, pungent and astringent in taste, such as asparagus and digestive spices.
- if you are Pitta predominant be very careful to control the amount of sour, salty and pungent tastes, which are all heat producing; sour fruits, such as tomatoes in particular, should be avoided along with yoghurt, hard cheese and hot spices.
- Vata types need plenty of sweet, sour and salty foods such as unrefined whole grains, organic milk and other dairy products, lentils and pumpkin, which are nourishing and anabolic (tissue building) in effect.

You also need to tailor your diet according to your particular idiosyncrasies such as any food intolerances, doshic imbalances you have been able to identify with the help of the dosha-finder questionnaire and your knowledge of your own personal digestive capacity.

At the end of this book you will find an extensive list of foods to enjoy and those to avoid, depending on your doshic balance.

Balancing agni (your digestive capacity)

We have already learned that good digestive power – or agni – is needed for us to stay healthy. Unfortunately, the typical Western diet is high in convenience and junk foods and we are all guilty of poor eating habits, such as 'eating on the run' or before our last meal has been fully digested. All these things upset our digestion by either increasing or weakening our digestive fire.

You can tell if your agni is weak because you probably suffer from a lot of gas or wind, may be constipated, and feel tired and heavy in the mornings and after a meal. If your agni is too high, you are likely to feel very thirsty, belch a lot, suffer from acidity, diarrhoea and general irritability.

To help keep your agni in balance, follow these simple guidelines:

- eat smaller, simpler meals

- when you have symptoms of weak agni, drink plenty of hot water with a dash of lemon
- get into the habit of drinking a cup of fresh ginger root tea after each meal
- season your cooking with digestive spices such as ginger, cumin and coriander.

Guidelines for Vata types

Follow this diet if you are Vata predominant, have detected a Vata imbalance using the dosha-finder, are suffering from symptoms such as nervous tension, insomnia, anxiety, bloating, constipation, painful or stiff joints and in late autumn/fall and winter when Vata is at its peak.

- Establish a routine of regular mealtimes. Ideally eat three to four meals a day.
- Take time out to eat in a calm environment and concentrate on your meal.
- Eat plenty of sweet, sour and salty-tasting foods as these are most nourishing.
- Favour foods that are warm, soupy and easy to digest. One-pot wonders such as soups and stews are great for Vata types.
- Avoid excesses of any kind; Vata people are prone to addictions such as alcohol, coffee and white sugar.
- Avoid fermented foods such as yeasted bread and beer.
- Limit your intake of very spicy and bitter foods such as coffee, chillies and uncooked apples as these aggravate the nervous system.
- Avoid raw, cold foods and frozen foods as much as possible, such as salads, dried fruits and ice cream.
- Never eat fried or greasy foods.

Dairy In their natural state all dairy products are good for Vata because they are sweet and nourishing. Organic dairy is best. If you are intolerant to cow's milk, rice and goat's milk products are healthy alternatives. It is best to drink milk on its own, warm and spiced with cardamom, cinnamon or cloves. Avoid ice cream, powdered and soya milk products. Hard cheeses should also be eaten sparingly as they are much harder to digest than soft cheeses. Yoghurt blended with water and spiced with ginger, cumin or other warming spices helps to pacify Vata (avoid yoghurt if you suffer from swelling or water retention). Butter and ghee are also good for Vata types, being nourishing and easy to digest.

Meat and fish Vata people need a steady supply of complete proteins in their diet because these build strength and stamina. If you are a meat eater, small amounts of white meat, fresh fish and venison are best, otherwise you can get what you need through a judicious balance of eggs and dairy products, supplemented by nuts and seeds. Combining grains with pulses – such as rice eaten with mung beans – is also a useful way to feed the body with complete proteins. Vata types should avoid pork, beef and lamb as they are simply too hard to digest.

Grains Wheat is the most nourishing and satisfying grain but is a common cause of allergies and is hard to digest because selective breeding over the past 100 years has greatly increased its gluten content. As a result, popular foods such as couscous, bulgar wheat and refined wheat products can be difficult for Vata types in particular to digest. Wholegrain, spelt and kamut varieties of wheat are the healthiest and most digestible forms available. Well-cooked basmati rice, oats, quinoa and amaranth are also good. Buckwheat, corn, millet and rye tend to be drying so, if you want to eat them, make sure you cook them with plenty of water and use butter, ghee or oil to balance their dryness. Avoid yeasted bread as it tends to ferment in the gut. If you must eat it then have it toasted!

Pulses These are the vegetarian's alternative to meat; however, although rich in protein, pulses are hard to digest. This means that Vata types should stick to the lighter varieties such as mung beans, red lentils, black lentils and marinated tofu. Cook them with plenty of warming, digestive spices such as turmeric, coriander seeds and cumin and eat them in small portions.

Vegetables Cooked rather than raw vegetables are best, especially asparagus, beetroot, carrots, turnips, parsnips, sweet potatoes, green beans, garlic and onion. Peas, green leafy vegetables, celery and summer squash are fine in moderation but should be cooked in oil or ghee and mildly spiced. Salads and leafy greens such as parsley, coriander leaf and spinach should only be eaten at lunchtime and then with a creamy or oily dressing. It is best to avoid brussels sprouts, cauliflower and cabbage as they promote wind. Also skip aubergines (eggplant), potatoes and raw tomatoes. If you suffer from stiff joints, it is particularly important to cut out tomatoes, potatoes and sweet peppers.

Fruits Most fruits are good for Vata, especially sweet, sour and heavy ones like apricots, berries, bananas, grapes, cherries, grapefruit, nectarines, oranges, lemons, limes, pineapples, fresh figs, peaches, melons, plums, mangoes and papayas. Raw apples and pears are too astringent but you can poach them with warming spices such as cinnamon and cloves. Avoid unripe and dried fruits (unless they are soaked), cranberries and pomegranates as they cause wind. Dried fruits, such as dates and figs, which have been soaked overnight are very nutritious. In winter it is best to eat fewer raw fruits; instead, try stewing or steaming them and spicing them with a little nutmeg or cinnamon.

Nuts and seeds All are good in moderation, especially almonds, but soak them in cold water overnight, then peel them in the morning as their skins can irritate the gut lining. Ten soaked almonds every morning gives the body enough nutrients for a whole day. Pumpkin seeds are good brain-food, but use sesame seeds with caution as they are very heavy to digest and gradually erode the natural tone of the GI tract. Avoid peanuts and all forms of salted nuts.

Oils All unrefined, cold-pressed oils are good for Vata people, especially sesame oil which has the capacity to penetrate deep into the tissues, nourishing and lubricating the body and nervous system. Used externally, coconut and sesame oils promote lustrous hair, while mustard oil is great for the skin.

Sweeteners Sweet tastes reduce Vata, so all sweeteners in moderation are beneficial, except refined white sugar which is highly toxic and addictive. If bloating is present, however, avoid all forms of sweeteners until it subsides.

Spices Virtually all spices – especially ginger, cumin, coriander and asafoetida – are good in small quantities because they are warming in effect. Vata people, however, are often tempted to use spices excessively in the hope that this will improve their digestion; in reality this eventually aggravates Vata dosha so should be avoided! Vata-Pitta types in particular should be cautious because their addictive nature starts to crave spices while Pitta is seriously aggravated by their hot qualities.

Drinks All drinks should be served at room temperature or above and never iced. Avoid coffee – it is too stimulating and addictive. Instead, drink plenty of warming and soothing herbal teas such as chamomile, fennel, licorice and ginger. Wine is okay with or after a meal but avoid beer because of its yeast content. Vegetable and fruit juices are very nourishing for Vata types but should be consumed on their own like a small meal and not when suffering from a cough, cold or accumulation of mucus.

Guidelines for Pitta types

This is the diet to follow if you are Pitta predominant, suffer from any Pitta-related conditions such as skin inflammation or irritation, duodenal ulcer or fever, and in the summer months when Pitta flares up.

The key rules are to:

- avoid hot and spicy foods, which are typically sour, salty and pungent to the taste, particularly tomatoes and sour or unripe fruits; if you must eat them occasionally then have them as your evening meal rather than at lunchtime when Pitta is at its height.
- favour sweet, bitter and astringent tastes which are cooling and refreshing.
- limit your intake of alcohol, black tea, meat, eggs and salt .
- eat three meals a day; you can snack occasionally but allow at least four hours to elapse after your previous meal before doing so.
- include raw foods, fresh fruit and vegetable juices in your diet but do not consume them in combination with cooked foods
- never eat fried or greasy foods.

Dairy Sweet dairy products such as organic milk, unsalted butter and ghee are all excellent for pacifying heat. Avoid soured dairy products such as yoghurt, buttermilk and sour cream. Hard cheeses should only be eaten very occasionally, but soft cheeses are fine in moderation.

Meat and fish Although Pitta people have the power to digest meat, according to Ayurvedic wisdom meat-eating encourages aggression and irritability so is best avoided if possible. If you do eat meat, then chicken, turkey and venison are the best options. Seafood tends to cause allergies and – as Pitta types are prone to allergic reactions – should be avoided. If you do choose to eat fish, then freshwater varieties are preferable as they are less less salty and 'hot' in potency.

Grains Barley is the grain of choice because it is cooling, drying and actually reduces acidity levels in the stomach. Basmati rice, oats, quinoa and spelt wheat are the next best options. It pays to avoid yeasted bread which has a tendency to ferment in the gut; instead, make unyeasted bread a staple part of your diet.

Pulses Having a strong digestion, Pitta types can make a meal of hard-to-digest pulses; however, overconsumption causes acidity so, like most foods, it is best to eat pulses in moderation.

In small amounts all except kidney and butter beans are good for Pitta, with red, yellow and black lentils, mung beans and tofu topping the list. Chickpeas must be very well cooked or eaten as humous.

Vegetables Eat them in abundance, especially asparagus, broccoli, brussels sprouts, cabbage, fresh coriander, cucumber, cauliflower, celery, watercress, green beans, leafy greens, lettuce, mushrooms, peas, parsley, potatoes, pumpkin, sprouts, squashes and courgettes. Sour fruits and vegetables, especially tomatoes and bell peppers, must be avoided in all forms as their acid-producing qualities severely aggravate Pitta. This means cutting tomato-based pasta dishes from your diet entirely, but if you cook sweet peppers very slowly for 40+ minutes and add a little unrefined sugar this reduces their aggravating qualities, making them a healthy alternative to tomato-based sauces. When cooked, garlic and onion become sweet so are beneficial, but do be aware that they are too pungent to eat raw.

Fruits The basic rule is to favour sweet fruits and avoid the sour-tasting ones such as oranges, grapefruits and pineapples. Lemons are fine in moderation. Any unripe fruit is likely to be sour. The best fruits to choose are apricots, avocados, cherries, coconut, dried fruits, figs, dates, grapes, mangoes (in moderation), melon, nectarines, peaches, pears, plums and pomegranates when they are in season.

Nuts and seeds In general, these are too hot and oily for Pitta people although safflower, sunflower and pumpkin seeds can be eaten occasionally.

Oils Olive, sunflower and coconut oils are the best. Use them in small amounts as Pitta dosha is already slightly oily in nature. A healthy substitute is to get into the habit of cooking with ghee rather than oil. Ghee is particularly beneficial for Pitta types.

Sweeteners All natural sweeteners are good in moderation, except honey and molasses.

Spices Use more cooling herbs and spices such as fresh coriander leaves, aniseed, dill, cumin and fennel. Small amounts of black pepper and ginger are okay but hot spices must be avoided, particularly mustard, cayenne, paprika, fenugreek and cloves.

Drinks Aloe vera juice and cooling herbal teas made with mint, hibiscus and coriander should be taken daily. It's best to drink aloe vera juice in the morning on an empty stomach and 15 minutes before you eat any breakfast. Black tea is astringent so is suitable for Pitta types, but avoid coffee, it is too pungent and irritates the liver. Fresh fruit and vegetable juices are also good when taken on an empty stomach or at least three hours after your previous meal.

Guidelines for Kapha

Follow this diet if you are Kapha predominant, in late winter and early spring when Kapha is at its height, or if you have a Kapha-related ailment such as sinusitis, lung congestion, a sluggish digestion, fatigue, mucus problems, high cholesterol, water retention and cellulite.

- Above all, avoid overeating and eating too late at night.
- Kapha types really only need two meals a day, so you can afford to skip breakfast altogether or make it a nutritious fresh vegetable or fruit juice.
- Eat only when you are hungry and avoid the temptation to snack between meals!
- Increase the proportion of bitter, pungent and astringent-tasting foods in your diet. These tend to be light, dry and warming in nature, so combat fluid retention and congestion in the body.
- Reduce the amount of sweet, sour and salty-tasting foods and avoid all fatty foods such as crisps, biscuits and cakes.
- A largely vegetarian diet is recommended. If you eat meat, make sure you follow it up with some brisk exercise to speed up your metabolism and help the digestion process.
- Avoid cold and raw foods, which are heavier to digest.
- Avoid all iced and cold drinks.
- Never eat fried or greasy foods.
- Chew a slice of fresh ginger marinated in lemon juice before each meal to kick-start your digestive enzymes.
- Make sure you drink plenty of hot water and spicy herbal teas, especially ginger tea after your meals.

Dairy Having similar qualities to those of Kapha dosha, dairy products increase mucus levels so should be eaten sparingly. Products made from organic goat's milk are best; being lighter than cow's milk they are easier to digest. Always boil milk and spice it with cardamom or ginger before drinking it. A little ghee is fine, or use flaxseed oil as an alternative. Avoid very sour and dense dairy products such as yoghurt, ice cream and sour cream.

Meat and fish Being naturally well-nourished, Kapha people do not need meat, but if you enjoy it then opt for the lighter varieties such as turkey, chicken and venison and eat these sparingly. Seafood is okay in moderation but make sure you dry-roast, grill, broil or bake flesh foods rather than frying them.

Grains Kapha people need to eat fewer grains than other constitutional types because all grains are heavy in nature and so are bulk promoting. The best grains to choose are hot and drying varieties such as buckwheat, millet, quinoa, barley and corn. Favour brown basmati rice over white. Try to avoid wheat products altogether, especially pasta made from durum wheat. Most supermarkets and health food stores now have a wide range of wheat-free pastas so this does not mean cutting it out of your diet entirely! Any bread should be wheat-free and toasted first. Some tasty options include rye bread, sour dough and spelt wheat breads.

Pulses These are a better source of protein for you than meat but, again, only eat them in small amounts. Tofu, black beans, mung beans, pinto beans, red lentils and tofu are the healthiest choices. Avoid the heaviest varieties, namely soya beans, black lentils and kidney beans. Get into the habit of cooking pulses until they are very soft before eating them.

Vegetables As a general rule, all vegetables are good except for very juicy, sour and sweet varieties such as cucumber and tomatoes. The best vegetables are leafy greens, red peppers and those containing seeds such as pumpkin and squash. Being very earthy, root vegetables are best eaten in moderation and potatoes should be avoided. The best way to cook vegetables is lightly steamed or stir-fried.

Fruits Go for the lighter fruits such as apples, pears, apricots, cranberries, mangoes, peaches and pomegranates. Dried fruits that have been soaked overnight in a little water are also good. Limit your intake of heavy, sweet, sour and very juicy fruits such as oranges, bananas, pineapple, figs and dates. Bananas are very heavy and cold in potency and so are best avoided. Never mix fruit with dairy products.

Nuts and seeds Basically, avoid them all – they are just too oily!

Oils Use as little oil as possible. Flaxseed, almond, corn and sunflower oils are the best options available.

Sweeteners Sweet tastes aggravate Kapha so avoid all sweeteners except honey, which has a drying effect on the tissues of the body. Two teaspoons of raw honey a day helps to reduce

Kapha qualities and is a great remedy for coughs, colds and lung congestion in general. Never heat honey above 40 degrees centigrade as it then becomes toxic.

Spices and condiments All spices are good, but avoid using too much salt as this absorbs moisture, which is bad news for Kapha types who tend to suffer from water retention, cellulite and oedema.

Drinks Herbal teas made with warming spices, such as ginger, cinnamon and clove, are great for Kapha people. Most good supermarkets and health food shops now offer a wide variety of Ayurvedic herbal teas, so check the ingredients and choose the ones that are warming and stimulating. If you drink alcohol, it is best to avoid beer and drink only wine or diluted spirits. The occasional cup of coffee and black tea can also be enjoyed.

Weight-loss diet

This kapha-balancing diet is suitable for anyone wanting to lose weight as most weight problems are due to a Kapha imbalance. Follow the general guidelines and, in particular, get into the habit of:

- having a nutritious, freshly made juice for breakfast such as carrot and apple juice with a bit of fresh ginger root – and nothing else.
- chewing a strip of fresh ginger root marinated in lemon juice before each meal.
- making lunch your main meal and not eating after 7p.m.
- being mindful of what and how you are eating; chewing each mouthful well and eating more slowly will help you to avoid overeating as it gives your brain more time to register that your tummy is being filled.
- going for a walk after your meal to help digestion.

Guidelines for dual constitutional types

The rule of thumb is to follow the diet that counteracts the controlling dosha for each season – Pitta in summer, Vata in autumn/fall, Kapha in spring – and to favour those taste factors that are balancing to both the doshas dominant in your constitution, for example:

- Vata-Pitta types need a Vata-controlling diet in autumn/fall and winter, and a Pitta diet in spring and summer. Sweet tastes should prevail because they balance both Vata and Pitta. Pungent tastes antagonize both doshas so should be avoided if possible.
- Pitta-Kapha types need to follow a Pitta diet from late spring to early autumn and a Kapha diet from late autumn to early spring. Bitter and astringent tastes balance both doshas, while sour and salty tastes should be avoided.
- For Vata-Kapha types it is slightly harder to strike the right balance because these two doshas are virtually opposite in nature. However, both are balanced by heat, so go for the three 'hot' tastes: sour, salty and pungent. In summer and autumn/fall use more sour and salty tastes to reduce Vata. In winter and spring, pungent tastes help to minimize the impact of Kapha.

Use the food properties chart provided earlier in this chapter to identify the principal taste factors of the foods you eat so that you can design yourself a diet that is healthy for your particular needs and the time of year.

Eating to suit the time of day, year and life

It is important to adapt your diet to suit the seasons, stages of life and also the time of day. The next chart shows which dosha is in control according to the progress of time. You can use it to help you plan your dietary programme.

Dosha	Season	Time of life	Time of day
Kapha	Late winter and spring	0–16 years	6a.m.–10a.m. 6p.m.–10p.m.
Pitta	Summer	16–55 years	10a.m.–2p.m. 10p.m.–2a.m.
Vata	Autumn/fall and early winter	55+ years	2a.m.–6a.m. 2p.m.–6p.m.

For instance, if you want to eat salads it's best to do so in the middle of the day when Pitta is at its peak. In the evening, when

Kapha rules, it is best to avoid eating cold, heavy, mucus-producing foods such as ice cream and yoghurt.

In childhood, Kapha predominates, which explains why children are predisposed to excess mucus and congestive disorders such as coughs and colds. This natural proclivity can be counter-balanced by ensuring your childrens' diets have a healthy balance of all six tastes and limiting the amount of mucus-producing foods such as yoghurt and ice cream. In adulthood, Pitta takes control so we need to increase our intake of sweet, bitter, astringent tastes to counteract its effect. Once we hit 55 years of age our bodies start to degenerate and dry out due to the increasing influence of Vata dosha. We need to increase our intake of nourishing, tissue-building foods at this time of life, such as hearty soups and stews.

Similarly, each season is governed by a particular dosha. The summer heat aggravates fiery Pitta; the cool, windy weather of autumn stirs up Vata; while Kapha takes control in the warm, moist months of spring. In the next chapter you will learn how you can tailor your diet to suit changes in the season.

Healthy eating habits

How you eat is just as important as what you eat! Your food can be of the best quality and perfectly suited to your nature but if you do not prepare and consume it in a wholesome way you can still compromise your health. This is why Ayurveda puts great emphasis on healthy eating habits. Like most things Ayurvedic, these 'rules' are plain common sense and much of the advice mirrors the basic good table manners we were taught as a child, such as eating at the table and chewing our food properly, but which may have fallen by the wayside due to the pressures of modern life.

Let's face it, after a long day we have all succumbed to the lure of a TV dinner, or gulped down our meal without a thought before dashing off to do something else. These are not healthy habits. A survey recently found that children who habitually watched TV while eating their meal ate a third more than they would otherwise. Focusing on our food while we eat actually helps us to avoid overeating and overloading our digestive system.

So, what are the healthy eating habits we need to adopt and what behaviour do we need to avoid?

Dos

- Eat to suit your constitutional type, likes and dislikes.
- Include a balance of all six tastes.
- Favour foods that are fresh and in season. This helps you to get the right nutrients for the time of year.
- If you can afford it, go organic; it cuts down on toxins and is better for the environment.
- Chew some fresh ginger root to wake up your taste buds and get the digestive enzymes flowing before you start your meal. You can prepare it by slicing it into long thin strips and marinating it in lemon juice with a pinch of rock salt.
- Favour freshly cooked food rather than pre-packed and convenience foods.
- Minimize the use of leftovers, tinned, frozen or preserved foods. Stale and highly processed foods cause ama to build in the GI tract.
- Eat only when you are hungry.
- Allow at least three to four hours between meals. Eating before your previous meal has been digested causes digestive upsets such as bloating, gas and heartburn and builds ama.
- Sit at the table and give each meal your full attention. That means not eating in front of the TV, computer or while you are reading. Focusing your complete attention on your food will help you to avoid overeating and promotes good digestion.
- Eat slowly, chewing each mouthful well (at least 30 times if you can!). This stimulates the digestive enzymes.
- Leave some space for digestion to take place! Fill your stomach half full of solid food, a quarter full of liquid and leave a quarter empty. An easy way to measure this is by cupping your two hands together, this equals the amount of solid food that's right for you. A single cupped hand is the right volume of fluid to take in one sitting. Our hands are designed to reflect our natural food capacity.
- Eat your evening meal as early as possible. Eating too late at night is a common cause of constipation and indigestion. When you go to sleep on a full stomach the food remains there undigested, which is why you tend to feel bloated, heavy and lethargic the next day.
- If you are a regular meat eater, take a short walk a little while after your meal to help the digestion process.

- When you travel, adjust your diet slowly as the change in water, food and climate can upset your digestion.

Don'ts

- Don't mix incompatible foods, such as dairy foods with fruit, fish with milk, fresh melon with any other type of food.
- Don't eat fruit or drink fruit juices with a meal. They need to be eaten on their own and at least three hours after your last meal.
- Avoid eating raw and cold foods straight from the fridge as their coldness depletes the digestive fire.
- Avoid iced drinks at all times; they extinguish the digestive fire. Always serve your drinks at room temperature or above.
- Don't eat when you are angry, depressed, emotionally upset or immediately after exercise as your digestive fire will be weakened at this time. Instead, wait until your appetite returns before eating anything.
- Avoid all Kapha-producing foods such as melon, yoghurt, cheese and ice cream in the evening.
- Avoid snacking between meals.
- Don't drink too much fluid while you are eating; this dilutes the digestive enzymes, allowing ama to form.
- Avoid fried foods of any kind; they aggravate all three doshas.

Preparing your food

Cooking with care and concentration is one of the common casualties of the modern way of life. Ayurveda teaches us that how we prepare and present our food is as important as what we choose to eat. The ritual of meal preparation is like a form of meditation, so try to put these simple guidelines into practice.

- Choose the freshest, purest food products you can afford to buy. If you can, go organic and/or bio-dynamic. If you eat meat, ensure that it has been farmed with care and consideration for the animals.
- Put all your love, energy and concentration into preparing each meal. Pour your hopes and wishes into your food as you chop, stir, mix and blend.
- Avoid the use of microwaves. Recent experiments show that microwave cooking actually changes the molecular structure of the foods we eat, converting them into amino acids that are known toxins to the liver, kidneys and our nervous system.

- Say a blessing before you eat. It need not be religious, just a simple 'thank you' for the food you enjoy every day.
- Eating is a sensory experience. Pay attention to the way your food is presented so you nourish your sense of sight, inhale the aromas to nourish your sense of smell and savour each mouthful so you really enjoy the flavours of your food. Savouring your food in this way will also help you to avoid overeating!
- Try not to talk too much while you are eating; instead, focus your full attention on your food.
- When you've finished, don't undo all the healthy living practices you've made such an effort to achieve by washing up with harmful chemical detergents. Use an environmentally friendly washing-up liquid and add a few drops of mandarin essential oil to lift your senses.

The importance of food combining

Different types of food need different digestive enzymes to be properly processed and assimilated. If we feed ourselves incompatible foods or too great a variety of food types in one sitting our body gets confused and fails to produce the enzymes necessary to fully digest our meal. This leads to fermentation, the formation of ama and improper nourishment, with symptoms such as intestinal gas, abdominal pain and swelling. If incompatible foods are eaten over a long period of time some form of illness will inevitably develop. This is why Ayurveda teaches us not to mix certain foods.

Milk, for example, is best eaten on its own. Consider the fact that all other mammals, even when they have been weaned, consume milk separately from other food substances. In particular, milk should not be combined with fish, meat, bananas, sour fruits or yeasted breads. Similarly, yoghurt should not be taken with sour fruits, hot drinks and mango.

Generally, fruits should be eaten on their own, especially melons, because they monopolize the digestive enzymes, making it impossible for other foods to be digested at the same time which means they sit in the stomach, undigested, and ferment.

Honey and ghee in equal proportions are toxic; however, in varying amounts, such as a ratio of 2:1 or 3:1, this combination is rejuvenating.

One-pot wonders such as soups and stews are a useful way to combine various food groups without causing any digestive upsets as the ingredients sort out their differences in the pot!

Many people who think they have a wheat intolerance find that it is actually the combination of bread made into a sandwich with cheese or meat (for example) that is incompatible for them and that, when eaten on its own, they can digest it without any difficulty.

Use your awareness to establish which combinations work for you and, as a general guide, try to eat simpler meals rather than a wide variety of different food groups in one sitting. Also, by cooking with warming digestive spices such as ginger, cumin and cinnamon you can improve your digestive capacity, making it easier for you to process combinations that would otherwise cause you problems.

Specific features of key food items

Many of the foods recommended by Ayurveda – such as wheat and dairy products – are considered 'taboo' by some people today. In fact, in their natural state these foods are still as wholesome and healthy as they were when Ayurveda originated more than 5,000 years ago; what makes these substances indigestible or aggravating is modern farming methods and food processing.

So, let's take a deeper look at the therapeutic effects and health issues related to key food items recommended by Ayurveda, such as ghee and honey, as well as some of the substances popular in modern diets, like coffee, tomatoes and white sugar.

Key therapeutic foods in Ayurveda

Milk has had a very bad press in recent years; however, used correctly, it is is an important part of a healthy, balanced diet. In its natural, unprocessed form milk is a powerful rejuvenator that builds tissue and immunity. Unfortunately, modern processing methods such as pasturization and homogenization change its chemical structure, making it toxic and indigestible for many people. It is essential, therefore, to purchase organic milk and to use it in the correct manner.

Being a complex and complete food, it is best to drink milk on its own and warmed to reduce its mucus-producing qualities and increase its digestibility. Ayurveda recommends drinking warm milk lightly spiced with digestive herbs such as turmeric, ginger, cardamom, cinnamon, nutmeg and cloves. It can also be mixed with ghee and honey for a more powerful rasayana effect, just make sure the ghee and honey are in ratios of three parts ghee to one part honey (or vice versa if you have a sweet tooth!) and that the milk is below 40 degrees centigrade when the honey is added. If you find that cow's milk is too heavy for you to digest properly then goat's milk and rice milk are good alternatives.

Ghee is clarified butter and is a staple part of any authentic Ayurvedic diet. It is particularly good for Vata and Pitta types, although Kapha people can also use it sparingly. The reason ghee is so beneficial is that its cooling and sweet properties build ojas and pacify Pitta dosha, while its oily quality stimulates the digestive fire.

Its lipophilic properties enable it to penetrate deeply into the cell membranes, making it a potent brain tonic that strengthens the nervous system, improves memory and concentration. Ghee also promotes a good complexion and eyesight. It has a very low fatty acid content and is rich in antioxidants such as vitamins A and E as well as vitamins D and K. In modern studies, ghee has also been found to increase good (HDL) cholesterol and decrease bad (LDL) cholesterol. Use it instead of unrefined cooking oils or take it on its own as a daily rasayana if you have a Vata- or Pitta-predominant constitution or if these doshas are aggravated in your system.

The best way to consume it for medicinal purposes is one tablespoon dissolved in a cup of hot water morning and night. If you are a Pitta type, add half a teaspoon of unrefined cane sugar to promote mental coolness. If you are Vata, add a teaspoon of honey to achieve a calmer, clearer mind.

Ghee is often used by Ayurvedic doctors as a vehicle for delivering herbal medicines because it carries these substances directly to the required site of action and increases their potency many times over. Common examples of medicated ghee include Shatavari ghee, Brahmi ghee and Triphala ghee. You may come across them if you consult an Ayurvedic specialist.

Honey is not just a tasty, natural food, it also has a powerful therapeutic action because of its ability to penetrate deep into the cells of the body without being digested. Externally it is an effective wound healer, especially when mixed in unequal

How to make ghee

Use a good quality, unsalted butter. It is best to prepare three or four pats of butter at a time. Place the butter in a pan and let it gently melt, then simmer over the lowest possible heat. At first it will make a bubbling noise, the butter will look thick and cloudy and foam will appear on the top. Stir it occasionally for the first five minutes then continue to simmer for a further 30–45 minutes. Slowly, particles will sink to the bottom of the pan and foam will settle on the top; in between, the pure butter oil will become clear. After 30–45 minutes, remove the pan from the heat, skim off the foam and discard it. Strain the clear liquid through a very fine sieve or piece of muslin into a jar and allow it to cool before sealing the container. Ghee has a very long shelf-life – in fact, the older it is the better – and does not require refrigeration.

proportions with ghee. Internally it is used as an aphrodisiac, to treat lung congestion, coughs and colds and as a cardio tonic because of its ability to reduce Kapha dosha. Eating locally produced honey can also protect you against seasonal allergies such as hayfever and asthma. When honey is heated above 40 degrees, however, it becomes toxic, so make sure you eat it in its raw state rather than cooked.

Salt is required for our bodies to perform essential biochemical functions, however, use it with caution if you are Pitta or Kapha predominant or if these doshas are aggravated. Too much salt in our diet makes the blood thick and viscous, leading to problems such as hypertension. Rock salt is the best form of natural salt and can be used in small quantities even when other salts are prohibited because it absorbs less water than other varieties, so does not block the channels of the body.

Rice is considered the king of grains in Ayurveda and is an important source of complex carbohydrates. Apart from wheat it is the most widely consumed grain in the world. Basmati rice is the best option because it is relatively light to digest while still being packed full of nutrients.

Wheat has been much denatured by modern farming methods which produce higher-yielding crops with a very high gluten content. Gluten is something many of us find hard to process. In its original form, however, wheat is still one of the best sources of nutrition available to us today. Take the time to seek out good quality sources of unrefined wholegrain, spelt or kamut wheat, which have a lower gluten content, to include in your diet. If you still find it hard to digest, barley is the most suitable alternative as it is both nourishing and cooling. Millet, quinoa, buckwheat and rye are useful alternatives but are more heating in their effect. A little trial and error will help you to establish which of these is best suited to your specific digestive capacity and mind–body type.

Healthy alternatives to common addictions

Coffee is one of the most common addictions today. Used regularly it overstimulates the nervous system, triggering tension and insomnia. It should therefore only be drunk infrequently and in small amounts by Kapha types, who need more stimulating substances to speed up their sluggish metabolism.

The good news is that there are now many delicious varieties of Ayurvedic herbal teas available on supermarket shelves as well as in specialist health food stores which you can use therapeutically to help your mind and body adjust to the daily and seasonal cycles of life. Use soothing brews to help you wind down at night, energizing blends to kick-start your day and cooling decoctions to take the heat out of your system in the middle of the day.

Alcohol dependency is another common health problem. Ayurveda teaches us that in small doses alcohol is like nectar, but taken to excess it is a powerful toxin because it impairs the function of our liver and brain. Alcohol dependency is often due to a craving for sweet tastes; sweet-tasting foods and drinks can therefore be used as substitutes. Wholegrains, for example, help to stabilize blood sugar levels, while fresh juices such as grape, pear and pure carrot juice can be used as 'quick fixes' to overcome alcohol cravings. Fresh coconut flesh steeped in a little hot water, blended, strained and then topped up with cold water is also an effective alcohol substitute.

White sugar has an effect on the body similar to alcohol. It intoxicates the mind and triggers cravings. It is an extreme example of food processing given that it lacks virtually all the metabolism-controlling minerals that were part of its original structure. In Ayurvedic terms, white sugar depletes the body of ojas. There are many healthy alternatives to white sugar nowadays, including raw cane sugar, solidified sugar-cane juice (jaggery), raw honey, barley malt, rice syrup, maple syrup and molasses.

Finally a word on **tomatoes**. While rich in vitamins A and C, the average modern diet has a very high proportion of tomatoes. Being sour, hot, light and juicy, tomatoes have the power to antagonize all three doshas when eaten to excess, especially Pitta and Kapha. The seeds and skin also aggravate Vata dosha. As a general rule, reduce the quantity of tomatoes in your diet and eat them in their cooked rather than raw state.

Summary

We've covered a lot of territory in this chapter so let's briefly recap on the key points.

1 Tailor your diet to suit your constitution, the time of day, year and your stage of life.

2 Fresh, seasonal, locally produced food is best. It has the right mix of nutrients for the time of year and cuts down on food miles so is better for our environment.

3 Freshly cooked food is better for you than leftovers and convenience foods.

4 Buy the best-quality foods you can afford in their natural state, such as wholegrains and organic dairy products.

5 How you eat is just as important as what you eat; remember to prepare your food and eat it with concentration and to chew your food properly!

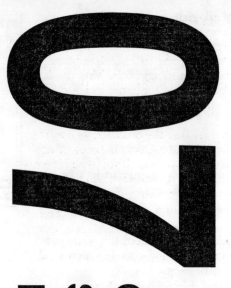

07

**daily and
seasonal
routines**

In this chapter you will learn:
- healthy living tips for your everyday life
- how to adjust your diet and lifestyle to suit the seasons
- simple yoga, therapeutic breathing and meditation practices you can start to apply.

The art of healthy living

One of the greatest gifts of Ayurveda is that it teaches us how to live in harmony with the rhythm of nature, through daily and seasonal lifestyle practices that take into account the fluctuations of our biological clock and changes in the world around us. By these means we can stay healthy and avoid those health problems to which we are most susceptible.

We learned in the previous chapter that the doshas take control not just in certain seasons, but also at particular times of day and stages of life. In this chapter we will learn wholesome lifestyle habits that you can cultivate to balance this effect and so improve your overall mental and physical wellbeing.

It may not be possible to build all of these recommendations into your daily lives, but if you can embrace the core principles and start to apply just a few of these practices – such as drinking a cup of hot water first thing in the morning rather than a cup of coffee – you will soon feel the benefits.

Whatever your nature, a disciplined routine of regular sleeping hours, waking, eating, exercising and waste elimination delivers major health benefits. It not only helps to regulate our bodily functions but also builds self-esteem and peace of mind.

A healthy daily routine

We have learned that each of the doshas dominates at a particular time of day (see figure 3 on page 114).

The creators of Ayurveda used this knowledge of the doshic clock to develop a healthy daily routine. Although conceived thousands of years ago, much of this advice is relevant today.

Don't worry if you do not have the time or opportunity to do it all! Just make a few changes and use your awareness to measure the benefits. The slightest improvement in your sense of wellbeing can be a powerful incentive for making more changes in the future.

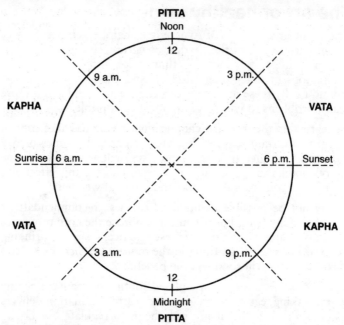

figure 3 The doshic clock

Morning routine

Getting off to a good start in the morning creates a sense of calm and control that can carry us through the most hectic of days. Similarly, if we oversleep and have to run for the train we tend to feel 'behind' and hassled for the rest of the day. This is why Ayurveda puts such emphasis on preparing our minds and bodies for the day ahead via a healthy morning routine.

At first glance this routine looks daunting. Indeed, critics of Ayurveda often argue that the time it takes to perform these tasks simply does not fit with the pace of modern life. In fact, these modern-day pressures make it all the more important for us to get off to a good start every day. Try to keep an open mind and gradually build these healthy living practices into your day.

Wake up early

Ideally, wake up just before sunrise everyday. This is the time of 'brahma murta', which translates as, 'the time of knowledge'. It is the point in time when our minds are at their most perceptive and also means we can enjoy the dawning of a new day. Waking up early gives us some quality time to spend on ourselves, preparing our minds and bodies for the day ahead. If you need another good reason for getting up a little earlier than normal, remember that this is the time of day when Vata – which is responsible for our waste elimination processes – takes control, so early rising helps to promote proper bowel movements. If you get up late and in a rush it is unlikely that your bowels will move, especially if you are Vata or have a Vata imbalance.

If you are Vata predominant, try getting up by 6a.m., Pitta by 5.30a.m. and Kapha by 5a.m. Even if you only achieve this once a week, do give it a try and notice how it increases your sense of vitality and control.

Drink a cup of hot water

Rather than starting your day with a shot of caffeine, ease your digestive system into life with a cup of hot water. This is a bit like washing a saucepan before cooking as it effectively rinses the stomach of any food residues left over from last night's meal. It also wakes up the digestive enzymes and kick-starts the peristalsis movement ready for the first meal of the day. People with constipation will find this a particularly useful habit to cultivate.

Exercise your senses

Splash your face and eyes with cold water in summer and autumn to reduce tension and tiredness. In winter and spring use lukewarm water.

Just as our bodies need exercise, so do our senses of perception. The yogic practice of palming is a great way to exercise the eyes. First, roll your eyes clockwise and then anti-clockwise five times. Then close them, rub your palms together vigorously and use them to cover your eyes while counting up to ten. Uncover your eyes and look straight ahead, keeping the eyes relaxed. Look up, down, to the right and to the left, then close your eyes again and repeat the palming process.

Gargle with warm water flavoured with a pinch of turmeric or, if you have a dry mouth, use pure ghee or licorice root powder to cleanse and moisten the mouth. Gargling daily exercises our facial muscles helping to prevent wrinkles and the signs of ageing.

Cleanse your sinuses by pouring a small amount of salted water into one nostril and expelling it out of the other nostril. You can use a small-spouted teapot to do this. Make sure you breathe through your mouth throughout the process to stop water from entering the upper part of your nasal passages. Alternatively, moisten your little finger with ghee or sesame oil and apply it into each nostril. This ancient practice cleanses the nasal passages of excess mucus, increases the circulation of blood to the brain, so boosting mental clarity, and combats the drying effect of central heating in winter.

Clean your teeth and tongue

Good oral hygiene is a key part of any morning routine. Remember to change your toothbrush regularly and use dental floss to prevent the build-up of bacteria.

Use a tongue scraper or spoon to cleanse your tongue of any white coating. This removes bacteria and helps to prevent bad breath. Scrape from the root to the tip of your tongue and repeat the process several times. If your tongue is heavily coated and your breath smells of last night's meal, skip breakfast and have a cup of hot water or ginger tea instead. It means your previous meal has not been fully digested. A short fast will help to cleanse your GI tract of any undigested foods.

Regulate your bowel habits

This is very important today. One of the reasons so many people suffer from constipation is that we do not take the time to train our bowels to empty at a regular time each day, before taking in more food! Even if you don't feel the urge, make this a part of daily routine and before too long your system will respond.

Self-massage

In Chapter 4 we looked in detail at the methods of self-massage, including the recommended base and essential oils for each constitutional type. Spend 10–15 minutes now putting this knowledge into practice. Remember that sesame oil is best for Vata types, sunflower for Pitta and corn oil or dry body brushing for Kapha types.

Massage has so many benefits. It not only improves the quality of the skin and reduces signs of ageing, but also works on the fabric of our minds and bodies by soothing Vata, improving circulation, reducing the build-up of lactic acid in the muscles, relieving muscle and joint pain, liquefying fat so helping to reduce cellulite, and calming the mind. Make sure you include your head and the soles of your feet whenever you massage. If you don't have ten minutes to spare on a full body massage then just oiling the soles of your feet helps to promote mental clarity and a sense of wellbeing.

Washing

Now take a shower or bath. In summer, Pitta types should wash in cold water. Washing in either hot or cold water is good for Kapha people (a cold shower speeds up the metabolism and helps to burn up fat). Vata people should wash with warm water. Avoid bathing within half an hour of eating as it draws the blood needed for digestion away from the GI tract.

Don't compromise your health by washing with soaps and hair products that contain harmful chemicals such as propylparaben. Instead, seek out the best organically produced products you can afford which are free from chemicals and artificial perfumes.

Take regular exercise

Exercise clears the channels of the body, eliminates toxins, releases endorphins, promotes good circulation, burns fat and builds immunity. It is particularly good for people with depression and mental health problems because the endorphins released are 'happy hormones', so soothe troubled minds.

Even if you don't have time for a full exercise routine you can always take a short walk or laugh! Laughing actually improves the functions of the lungs, burns calories, oxygenates the blood and releases endorphins.

Tailor your choice of exercise to suit your constitution:

- Kapha types need more vigorous exercise and should vary their routines to avoid becoming complacent! Aerobics, dancing and jogging are good options.
- Pitta people benefit from more moderate forms of exercise and should take care to choose activities that are not overly competitive, such as team sports, swimming and hiking.
- People with high levels of Vata are drawn to high-impact exercise like the proverbial moth to a flame. However, they really do need to follow gentle, more meditative practices

such as yoga, tai chi and pilates. Jogging in particular is not good for Vata types because of the strain it puts on their already vulnerable joints. Remember also that at 55 years of age we enter the Vata stage of life so need to practise less strenuous forms of exercise such as stretching, swimming and yoga.

As a rule, exercise to half your natural capacity, which is the point at which you break out in a light sweat.

Practise yoga

Whatever your mind–body type, 15–20 minutes of yoga a day will transform your mental and physical state.

Yoga is an integral part of an Ayurvedic way of life. As well as improving flexibility, physical strength and the functions of our organs, yoga has a powerful effect on our mind. By focusing your attention on achieving specific asanas (postures) you can quieten your mind, stopping the constant chatter of thoughts and ideas that cloud perception and cause stress. Practising yoga leads to a state of bliss similar to that achieved through the regular practise of deep meditation.

If you do nothing else, get into the habit of practising the 12-posture sun salutation given here. This cycle wakes up all the organs of the body, balances the chakras (energy centres) and invigorates the mind. Remember to regulate your breathing while doing this sequence of postures.

The sun salutation (surya namaskara)

Posture 1: Stand up straight, with your feet together and your palms pressed together in front of your chest; inhale slowly.

Posture 2: On the next exhalation, arch backwards with your head between your arms.

Posture 3: Inhale and fold your body forward into a deep forward bend. Aim to get your palms flat on the ground on either side of your feet. If you are not used to doing this be patient! It will take time for your body to achieve the levels of flexibility needed to reach your toes.

Posture 4: As you exhale, draw your right leg back and look up.

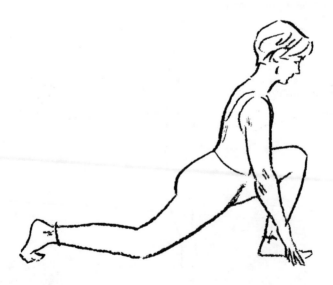

Posture 5: Inhale as you bring your left leg back to meet your right and then hold your breath while you are in the plank pose.

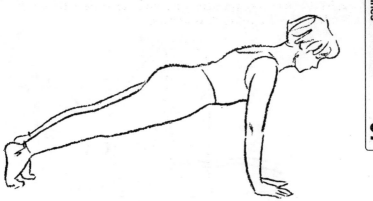

Posture 6: Exhale slowly and drop first your knees, then your chest and finally your chin to the floor leaving the buttocks and lower abdomen raised.

Posture 7: Inhale and arch up in the cobra posture, keeping your chin up, hips and toes on the floor and elbows bent.

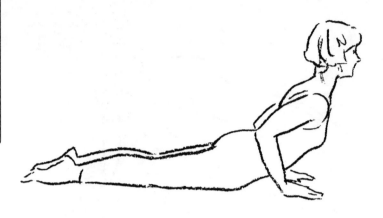

Posture 8: Exhale, curl under your toes and draw yourself up into a triangle, pushing upwards into your buttocks while making sure your neck stays in line with your spine. Breathe easily for one or two breaths.

Posture 9: Inhale and draw your right leg forward between your hands and look up.

Posture 10: Exhale slowly as you bring your left leg to join the right with your knees straight. Fold down into a forward bend as you did at the beginning, with your hands on either side of your feet. Inhale and exhale gently.

Posture 11: On the next inhalation stand up and arch backwards with your head between your arms.

Posture 12: Exhale and return to the position of namaste with your palms pressed together in front of your chest.

Repeat this process, leading with your left leg this time, to complete one round. Ideally, Vata people should perform 12 rounds and hold each posture for the count of two breaths, Pitta types should do 15 rounds and Kapha people up to 20 rounds. Notice how relaxed, energized and clear-headed you feel at the end of this practice.

One of the beauties of yoga is that it is a totally portable form of exercise which requires no equipment other than your own body! This means you can practise it 'anytime, anywhere', making it a great habit to cultivate if you travel a lot with your job.

Over the next few pages you will find illustrations for all the yoga postures recommended in this chapter. You can use these to get started, but finding a good yoga teacher is the best way forward if you want to make yoga a part of your life.

Useful asanas for Vata types

If you are a Vata type you need to practise postures that are calming, grounding and supportive. There are many types of yoga. The schools best suited to your constitutional type include Raja yoga, Kripalu yoga, Gyana yoga, Bhakti yoga and Satyananda yoga. The following postures are good to practise.

- **Standing postures:**

tree pose

triangle

warrior pose 1

warrior pose 2

warrior pose 3

• **Inverted postures:** shoulder stands are great for Vata types because they nourish the brain and balance the thyroid gland. Support your shoulders on a block to allow space for the neck and throat to stretch gently with the breath.

Avoid this posture when you are menstruating.

- **Seated postures:**

boat pose

spinal twist

forward bend

hero pose

easy cross-legged pose

- **Back bends:**
  bridge pose

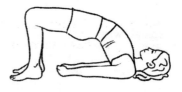

- **Relaxing postures:** get into
  the habit of practising the
  corpse position for 20
  minutes every day if you
  can as it is the best way for
  you to truly relax your
  whole body. Placing a
  lavender bag over your eyes
  will help you to relax.

Useful asanas for Pitta types

Pitta types need to practise postures that are cooling, balancing and relaxing. Seek out yoga schools such as Raja yoga, Satyananda, Iyengar, Ghyana and Bhakti yoga.

While the sun salutations are always good to practise, if you are Pitta you might like to try doing moon salutations instead.

In addition, the following asanas are recommended.

- **Standing postures:** forward bend (see p. 127)

eagle pose

wide-leg forward bend

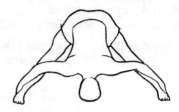

half-moon pose

- **Inverted postures:**

the plough

downward-facing dog

- **Back bends:**

cobra pose

camel pose

- **Seated postures:**

half or full lotus

child's pose

pigeon pose

squat pose in namaste

spinal twists when lying down

- **Relaxing postures:** practise the corpse pose for 15 minutes a day while listening to calming mantras or the sounds of nature from a CD.

Useful asanas for Kapha types

If you are Kapha you need to pick up the pace with more motivating, stimulating and energizing postures. You will get the most benefit by practising Ashtanga, Iyengar, Bikram or Karma yoga. The following postures are particularly good for Kapha people.

- **Standing postures:**
  warrior pose numbers 1
  and 2 (see page 126)

  chair pose

  dancer pose

  revolving triangle

- **Inverted postures:**

  handstand

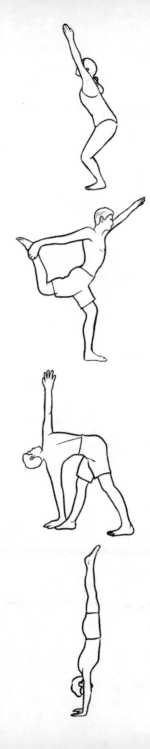

headstand

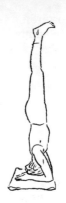

peacock pose

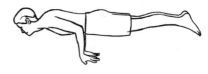

- **Back bends:**

upward-facing dog

bow pose

wheel pose

- **Seated postures:**
  boat pose (see page 127)

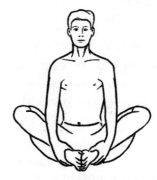

soles of feet touching

lion pose

cow face pose

Practise pranayama (therapeutic breathing techniques)

After your morning exercises, spend a few minutes practising some controlled breathing techniques. This energizes and focuses the mind and body and is particularly useful in times of stress. When we are stressed we tend to breathe too shallowly. Even when we breathe normally, we only expel about two-thirds of the air from our lungs. The other third remains there, stagnating. Practising therapeutic breathing techniques enables us to expel more stagnant air from the lungs, removing carbon dioxide and flooding our bodies with life-giving oxygen. As a result, it is a practice that alleviates symptoms of nervous tension and anxiety as well as expanding the mind.

Abdominal breathing is a very simple practice to start with.

- Lie on your back, relax your limbs completely and gently rest your hands on your abdomen with the fingertips touching.
- Breathe in through your nose, expanding your stomach completely, like a balloon filled with air. Your fingers will part as your abdomen expands.
- Hold your breath for a second or two and then breathe out slowly letting your stomach relax fully. Your fingers should now be touching again.
- Repeat this process for five to ten minutes and then take a few moments to notice how clear and energized your mind and body feel.

This method of breathing gently massages your internal organs and improves the flow of blood to the muscles and nerve centres. As you become more adept at it, try inhaling to the count of four, retaining the breath for a moment, and then exhaling to the count of eight. This helps to eliminate more stagnant air and carbon dioxide from the lungs.

Alternative nostril breathing is recommended for all constitutional types, particularly Vata, because it balances both the right and left sides of the brain. Shitali pranayama (cooling breath) is good for Pitta because it cools the entire body. Kapalabhati (purifying breath) is good for Kapha types because it dislodges excess mucus and improves overall lung capacity. In the next chapter you will find a step-by-step guide on how to practise these methods of pranayama.

Practise meditation

People are often wary of meditation because they see it as a complex art. While it does take self-discipline and regular practice to reap the benefits, meditation is simply the ability to quieten the constant chatter of your mind through peaceful contemplation. It's a bit like meeting an old friend, a little awkward at first but ultimately a rewarding and uplifting experience.

Regular practice of just 15 minutes a day delivers a sense of calm and clarity that can carry you through the most stressful of days. That's because meditation has been found to stimulate hormones similar to the endorphins we release during exercise, to lower blood pressure, improve concentration, reduce anxiety, fatigue, nervousness and stress. It works by cleansing our subconscious mind of negative influences and calming the central nervous system. Practised daily, meditation removes destructive impulses and opens up new insights, creativity and awareness.

In the next chapter we will explore various different techniques you might like to try out for yourself but, for now, let's stick to a very simple exercise you can use to get started.

When you are ready to meditate, find a quiet place to practise and settle yourself into a comfortable sitting position – either kneeling, sitting cross-legged or on a chair with your spine straight. Rest your hands on your knees, palms up, with your index finger and thumb touching.

Begin by breathing slowly and deeply from your abdomen and then focus your full attention on an object, such as a lighted candle, or close your eyes and visualize a beautiful image such as the sun, a waterfall or a lush green garden in your mind. Choose the technique that works best for you.

Don't worry that thoughts keep popping into your head; just gently push them away and re-focus your mind on your meditative practice. Little by little you will find it easier to stop the noise of your mind and slip into a soothing meditative state.

Breakfast

Use the dietary advice from the previous chapter to make a breakfast that's healthy for you and suited to the time of year, such as a warming bowl of porridge made with rice milk and sweetened with maple syrup or honey in the winter, or a plate of fresh fruit in the summer. Remember to eat only if you are hungry and your previous meal has been fully digested. Kapha types are best skipping breakfast altogether or drinking a fresh fruit juice such as a blend of apple and carrot with some fresh ginger root.

Work

The ancient Ayurvedic texts advise us to choose a profession that is noble, respected and pleasurable. While this is not always possible you can manage the way you approach your work. Try to carry the clarity of mind you have gained from your morning's preparations into the workplace. Remember also to practise ethical conduct and any other relevant methods of mind control mentioned in the previous chapters.

Lunchtime routine

Ideally make lunch your main meal. It is the time of day when Pitta is strongest, which means our digestive power is at its peak, so you can afford to enjoy a hearty lunch and even include some raw foods and salads at lunchtime. It's advisable for Vata and Pitta types to eat around noon and Kapha slightly later, between 1p.m. and 2p.m. but do remember to eat *only* if you are hungry not simply because it is lunchtime!

It is very important to find time and space to concentrate fully on your meal rather than gulping it down in front of a computer, reading the paper or while you are doing something else. Even if you can only snatch 15 minutes, make sure you do so and give your food your undivided attention. Remember to practise the healthy eating habits mentioned in the previous chapter, such as chewing each mouthful properly.

Try to avoid eating sandwiches and fast foods. Instead, go for meals that are freshly made and less complex to digest, such as nourishing soups in winter and leafy green salads in summer. Also make sure you don't drink too much during the meal as it dilutes your digestive enzymes, hindering the digestive process. If possible, take a short walk after eating to aid your digestion.

Napping in the daytime

Sleeping in the daytime is not usually advisable, although Vata types can benefit from a quick ten-minute snooze in the afternoon. Kapha people, however, should avoid the temptation to sleep during the day as it slows their already sluggish metabolism.

Evening routine

Eat as early as you can. Traditionalists advise Vata types to eat at 6p.m., Pitta types between 6p.m. and 7p.m. and Kapha types between 7p.m. and 8p.m. Just do what you can to give your body as much time as possible to digest your meal before going to bed.

The tendency in the Western world is to save the largest meal of the day for last. This is not a healthy habit. Make lunch your main meal and eat more sparingly at night. Ideally take a short walk after your meal. Then you can take time out to do the things you enjoy in the evening, such as watching TV.

Bedtime routine

Rather like a child, the best way to get a good night's sleep is by following a regular routine. Avoid stimulating activities such as watching TV just before going to bed. Instead, rub a little oil into the soles of your feet to relax you and maybe practise some meditation or your chosen mantra.

A cup of warm milk spiced with cardamom is a great habit to cultivate just before bed because it nourishes and soothes active minds.

Get into the habit of going to bed at a consistent and relatively early hour – this will help you to get up earlier! Vata types need more sleep than other types, ideally eight hours a night, so aim to be in bed by 10p.m. If you are a Pitta person around seven hours a night is ample, so go to bed between 10p.m. and 11p.m. While Kapha types can happily sleep for nine hours or more they need much less sleep than they are in the habit of having! Sleeping less speeds up the metabolism and helps to avoid weight gain. Ideally Kapha people should be in bed by midnight and sleep for only five hours. If you are Kapha predominant this will be a daunting prospect, but give it a try and see what works best for you.

Seasonal guidelines

Just as the hours of the day are ruled by Vata, Kapha and Pitta, so too are the seasons. To be at our healthiest, we need to adjust our way of life – from the clothes we wear to the foods we eat – to suit the changing qualities and features of the world around us.

These days the seasons are less predictable and weather patterns will vary depending on where you live in the world. Use your common sense to work out when is the right time for you to begin applying the seasonal guidelines provided here to your daily routine.

We often become ill at the junction of the seasons because our bodies have to adjust to the changing elements and weather patterns. Use the guidelines provided to gently ease your mind and bodies through this transition period. By making subtle and timely changes you can keep your body strong and avoid becoming ill.

Guidelines for spring

The slightly warmer, moist weather of spring liquefies Kapha that has built up in the body over the cold winter months. It's why we are so prone to coughs, colds, lung congestion and other mucus-related illnesses at this time of year. It is also the season when flowers start to shed their pollen, triggering hayfever and other allergies.

Following these basic guidelines will help you to stay healthy.

- Get up early, go for a brisk walk or do some yoga. If you can practise your yoga outside, do so! Increase your practice of those postures which open up the chest and hips, such as the half lotus, boat, lion and bow poses. The Bhastrika breathing routine (given in the next chapter) is a great practice in spring because it is so warming and energizing. Chanting out loud is also a good habit to foster at this time of year.

- Spring is the best time to detoxify your system. If you know a good Ayurvedic doctor, now is the time to get in touch and undertake Panchakarma. Alternatively you can do a home detox, either using the fasting method or the seven-day diet described in Chapters 4 and 5, or simply by following a juice fast of apple, pomegranate and/or berry juices for a week.

- Your diet should become lighter as the days become longer. Follow a kapha-pacifying diet by limiting your intake of heavy, oily, sweet, mucus-producing foods – such as ice cream and dairy products in general – and eating more light, pungent and astringent-tasting foods such as spring greens, cranberries, artichokes, celery, pulses and aromatic spices like ginger, black pepper and cayenne. If you eat meat, choose the lighter types such as chicken, turkey and venison.

- A cup of hot water with honey is great for digesting excess mucus and balancing Kapha dosha. Alternatively you can make a spicy brew using equal quantities of cumin, coriander and fennel seeds steeped in hot water.

- The colours we wear also have a therapeutic effect. In spring go for bright, cheerful, vibrant shades of gold, yellow, orange and red and avoid 'chilly' colours such as white, green and blue.

- Use candles, incense and essential oils scented with sweet, pungent fragrances that are stimulating and uplifting such as camphor, cinnamon, cloves, sage, thyme, cedar and frankincense.

- Don't be tempted to take a nap in the day whatever your constitution; it will make you feel slow and lethargic.

- Step up your exercise routine. Kapha types particularly need plenty of regular, vigorous activity such as jogging or aerobics at this time of year.

Guidelines for summer

The hot, dry, sharp qualities of summer aggravate Pitta. You need to take steps to reduce this, particularly if you are a Pitta type or have identified a Pitta imbalance using the dosha-finder.

- Follow a Pitta-pacifying diet by eating colder, sweet, bitter and astringent-tasting foods such as organic milk, cooling herbal teas of mint and coriander and sweet-tasting fruits that are in season such as pears, apricots, grapes, plums, watermelon and sweet berries. Increase your intake of fluids with plenty of cold, but not iced, drinks such as fresh lime juice mixed with water or a soothing lassi. Cold soups, salads and even ice cream are fine to eat at lunchtime, but in the evening lightly cooked foods are better. Limit your intake of meat to some chicken, turkey or prawns once a week and avoid red meat altogether as it is too heat inducing. Avoid sour fruits and those fruits and vegetables that are hot in potency, such as beetroot. If you are in doubt, check the qualities of the ingredients you want to eat with the food properties chart provided in the previous chapter.

Recipe for lassi

Simply blend two parts of plain, live yoghurt with four parts of water until it is creamy. Add a few drops of rose water if you like (available from most health food shops) or some cardamom seeds.

- Keep your alcohol intake down, especially if you are a Pitta type. A little white wine, spritzer or lager is okay, as are white spirits such as gin or vodka with a cooling mixer, but avoid heavier tipples such as rum, whisky and red wine.

- Cooling activities of all kinds are beneficial, such as a gentle stroll in the morning and evening when the sun is less intense. The ancient Ayurvedic texts recommend moonlight walks, taking cold showers or baths, drinking milk and wearing sweet-smelling perfumes that are cold in potency, such as lavender, jasmine, sandalwood, basil and rose.

- Certain gems and metals can actually have a cooling effect on the mind and body, such as sandalwood beads, pearls, moonstones and any form of silver jewellery.

- Wear calm, cooling colours that reflect the heat, such as white, green and blue. Avoid very sharp, stimulating colours like red, orange and yellow which are heat absorbing.

- Don't sit in the sun; it ages the skin, increases your risk of skin cancer and irritates Pitta!

- Make sure you cover up and wear loose-fitting clothes made of natural fibres, especially if you are a Pitta type who tends to sweat easily and whose skin generally freckles and burns easily.

- Keep your home and work environment well ventilated, allowing cool air to circulate.

- At this time of year more moderate forms of exercise are best, such as swimming and yoga. Continue with your sun salutations and build in some cooling postures such as the moon salutations and all types of forward bends. Pitta types should avoid inverted postures such as headstands and shoulder stands in summer. Meditating while chanting the om mantra is particularly good at this time of year.

- The cooling Shitali breath (given in the next chapter) is a great pranayama to practise in summer as are quiet, reflective forms of meditation. Try visualizing watery scenes such as a beautiful lake or the sea as part of your meditative practice.

- The warm summer months sap energy so you can afford to take a rest – and even a short nap – in the heat of the day.

- You can also go to bed a little later on summer evenings, around 11p.m. or midnight. Before going to bed, rub some coconut oil into the soles of your feet and place a few drops of sandalwood or lavender essence on your pillow.
- Keep sex to a minimum – it is too heat-producing and saps energy levels! When you do have sex try to time it for the early morning or evening when Kapha is at its peak and before Pitta takes control.

Guidelines for autumn/fall

The dry, cooler, windy weather of autumn/fall aggravates Vata, so at this time of year we need a steady supply of warm, nourishing experiences to combat its effect.

- Start your day early, around 5a.m. if you can, when the air is calm and the birds are still asleep. This will promote a sense of calm and clarity to carry you through your day.
- Continue with your yoga practice, emphasizing twisting and bending postures and increasing the number of repetitions if you can. Useful asanas for autumn/fall include the lotus, forward bends, back bends, spinal twists and the cobra. Inverted postures such as shoulder and headstands are also good in moderation. Keep practising your sun salutations.
- Alternative nostril breathing (given in the next chapter) followed by 10–15 minutes of meditation is a good habit to foster at this time of year.
- A quick massage with warm sesame oil – which is the best oil for pacifying Vata – is recommended for all types in the autumn/fall. Then take a nice, warm shower.
- Follow a Vata-pacifying diet of warm foods and sweet, nourishing tastes such as oatmeal porridge, rice and steamed vegetables, soups and stews. Avoid salads, raw foods and fasting as these will sap your strength.
- Take care to avoid stimulants such as black tea and coffee. Instead, drink plenty of warming, spicy herbal teas made with fresh ginger, cinnamon, clove and fennel, for example.
- You also need to avoid overstimulating activities such as listening to very loud music, driving too fast and vigorous exercise! All of these have the power to disturb sensitive Vata.
- Dress warmly and wear colours that are warming to the eye but not overly harsh, such as muted shades of gold, red, orange, yellow, white and whitish tones of green or blue.
- Use fragrances and essential oils that are sweet and calming,

such as sandalwood, rose, vertivert, lemongrass, lotus, lavender, gardenia, iris and honeysuckle.

- On windy days make sure you wear a hat and protect your ears to avoid Vata becoming disturbed.

- Warm, milky drinks are soothing, particularly at night. Now is the time to get into the habit of drinking a hot mug of milk lightly spiced with a pinch of ginger, cardamom and nutmeg at bedtime.

- Avoid naps during the day, unless you are a Vata type, and try to get to bed a little earlier now that the evenings are drawing in. Vata types in particular should be tucked up in bed by 10p.m.

Guidelines for winter

The cold, damp weather and cloudy skies increase Kapha dosha, although Vata can also be upset at this time of year. It is the season to wrap up warmly and eat plenty of nourishing, hot foods.

- In winter we can afford to conserve our energy by staying in bed a little longer, so there is no need to get up before 7a.m. Take your time and get up slowly.

- Keep practising your sun salutations and add in postures that stimulate the adrenal and pituitary glands, such as back bends and inverted postures.

- Now is the season to practise the Kapalabhati (purifying breath) or Bhastrika (heat producing breath) and to follow this up with some soothing alternate nostril breathing and a little meditation.

- After this, apply some warm sesame oil to your whole body and take a hot shower or bath.

- Choose fragrances and essential oils that are warm, pungent and uplifting, such as camphor, cinnamon, cloves, sage, thyme, cedar and frankincense.

- It's important to eat warm, cooked foods in winter and to get into the habit of drinking hot water throughout the day to loosen any toxins. Porridge makes a quick, nutritious breakfast while hot soups and stews, wholegrain bread and rice and steamed vegetables with a little ghee are good for lunch and dinner. Avoid uncooked foods.

- If you are a meat eater now is the time to indulge, because your digestion is at its strongest so you can afford to eat foods that are harder to digest.

- This is also the time of year when we can indulge in a little more alcohol. Red wine in particular is good for boosting circulation and digestion when taken before or after dinner.
- Dress warmly, favouring bright, cheery colours such as reds and oranges. Remember to wear a hat when you go outside as up to 60 per cent of our body heat is lost through our head!
- Avoid sleeping during the day as this builds Kapha dosha.
- Increase your levels of exercise. Vigorous exercise is heating and helps to prevent the build-up of mucus and congestion in the body.
- Winter is also the best time to indulge in sex, according to the sages of Ayurveda!
- The short, dark days can be lonely and depressing. We tend to hibernate as a result, which is a typical sign of Kapha taking control. Make the effort to surround yourself with good company; go out for dinner or to the cinema at this time of year.
- At the end of the day, rub a small amount of sesame oil into your scalp and feet to help soothe you to sleep.

08

breathing and meditation

In this chapter you will learn:
- about the eight limbs of yoga
- methods of breathing you can practise at home
- simple meditation techniques to get you started
- mantras to help you meditate.

The origins of pranayama and meditation

As we have already seen, yoga is an integral part of Ayurveda. Like Ayurveda it is a complete science that offers us much more than just physical postures to stretch our bodies. There are actually eight branches of yoga, as shown in the table below, of which pranayama and meditation are a part.

Yama	ethical conduct such as truthfulness and non-violence
Niyama	living with discipline and self-restraint; good personal hygiene, personal development and self-study, for example
Asanas	therapeutic postures that exercise the body and mind
Pranayama	controlled breathing techniques
Pratyahara	withdrawal from the sensory world – this form of meditation requires us to detach our minds from the stimulus provided by our senses of sight, hearing, taste, touch and smell; it frees us up from the physical world so we can start exploring our inner self
Dharana	focusing the mind on a single object such as a candle flame or a visual image in your head; it is another form of meditation and increases our self-awareness
Dhyana	meditation in the truest sense of the word, which is simply our ability to contemplate our inner self or consciousness creating space in the mind; it can be defined as a totally tranquil, non-resistant state of being
Samadhi	super-consciousness – this is the highest state of meditation and is very rare; it is only attained through sustained and devoted spiritual practice

We have already explored several of these limbs, such as the role of good conduct and personal hygiene in a healthy living regimen, and yogic postures we can use to strengthen our minds and bodies. Now we are going to look at the practices of pranayama and meditation in more detail and learn some simple exercises we can build into our Ayurvedic way of life. With daily practice, these two disciplines are hugely empowering. They help us to realize our full potential by creating a sense of inner strength, greater self-awareness and mental clarity; qualities that help us to handle the pressures of life with greater ease.

The best way to learn meditation and pranayama is with the help of a qualified teacher rather than from the pages of a book. It is hoped that the insights given here will motivate you to explore these powerful mental therapies further with the help of a trained professional. If you want to find a good local yoga teacher, get in touch with your national yoga industry association, such as the British Wheel of Yoga at www.bwy.org.uk.

The secrets of controlled breathing

The better we breathe the more effectively we nourish our minds and bodies, it is a simple as that! If you do nothing else with the knowledge you have gained from this book, get into the habit of controlling your breathing as it really does deliver tremendous health benefits.

We need oxygen to process our food, create energy, cool our bodies and for our brains to function properly. By breathing fully we exercise our lungs to their full capacity, flooding our cells and all the tissues of the body with life-giving oxygen and expelling carbon dioxide and other toxins. It is a process that reduces fatigue and improves concentration. Controlled breathing can even relieve physical problems such as headaches, asthma, bronchitis, high blood pressure, panic attacks and sinusitis, as well as reducing our risk of heart disease and slowing the ageing process.

Our breathing is also inextricably linked to our state of mind. Our brains actually need three times more oxygen than the rest of our organs to function properly. When we breathe more deeply, therefore, we nourish our brains, improving our mental capacity so we feel calmer, more alert and intellectually able.

If you practise pranayama daily you will quickly notice the health benefits in the terms of greater mental and physical strength, powerful new insights, an increased ability to resolve difficult emotions and a greater sense of happiness and wellbeing overall.

Various methods of pranayama are explained in this chapter, so you can pick and mix your practice to suit your specific emotional and physical needs at any given point in time.

Caution

Pranayama is a very powerful process and should be treated with caution if you suffer from health problems such as a heart condition, blood pressure problems or glaucoma. If in any doubt, consult your doctor or a trained practitioner.

Anulom lom (alternate nostril breathing)

This method of breathing is especially good for Vata types or whenever you feel anxious and stressed. By oxygenating both the right and left sides of our brain and purifying the subtle channels of our nervous system it promotes a sense of balance, clarity and calm.

1 Sit cross-legged, or on a chair with your feet flat on the ground if this is more comfortable for you. However you choose to sit, make sure your spine is completely straight (imagine a cord is pulling you up from the crown of your head to keep your spine upright).

2 Use your right thumb to close your right nostril and inhale deeply through your left nostril, breathing deep down into your belly rather than into your chest.

3 Hold your breath for a moment and then use the ring finger of your right hand to close your left nostril before exhaling deeply through your right nostril.

4 Inhale through the right nostril, hold, close your right nostril with your right thumb once again and then exhale through your left nostril.

5 Repeat this process, alternating between the left and right nostrils for five to ten minutes. Finish the practice by exhaling out of the left nostril.

6 When you have finished, give yourself a few moments to sit and relax with your eyes closed to appreciate the effect of this breathing on your mind and body.

Shitali (the cooling breath)

This breathing exercise is great for Pitta types and in the heat of summer as it has a cooling effect on the mind and body. It actually lowers blood pressure and improves our digestion and metabolism.

1 Sit comfortably, either cross-legged or on a chair, but again make sure your spine is completely straight. Rest your hands on your knees, palms facing up with your thumb and forefinger touching.

2 Curl your tongue into a tube and inhale slowly with your mouth open before exhaling slowly through your nostrils. (If you can't curl your tongue into a tube, just keep your mouth slightly open and allow the cool air on the inhalation to wash over your tongue and then breathe out through your nostrils).

3 Repeat this sequence for five to ten minutes.

Kapalabhati (cleansing breath)

This breath purifies the mind and body but should not be practised if you have high or low blood pressure, a hiatus hernia, any ear or eye problems or if you are pregnant. It cleanses the sinuses, massages the front part of the brain and strengthens the lungs and abdominal muscles while removing toxins from the base of the lungs. Stop the practice if you feel dizzy and then begin again, trying to maintain an even rhythm so that the gaseous exchange in the lungs returns to a state of balance.

If you are a smoker you may find you suffer from a slight headache after this practice as residual nicotine from the lungs is pushed into the blood stream. With frequent practice, however, this breath helps to cleanse the lungs of nicotine and any side effects will pass.

1 Sit comfortably, either cross-legged or on a chair, but make sure you keep your spine straight. Rest your hands on your knees, palms facing upwards with your thumb and forefinger touching.

2 Inhale through the nose then exhale sharply and forcefully through your nostrils contracting your abdominal muscles at the same time, so you expel the air held deep within your lungs.

3 Continue for 10–20 contractions to start with and only increase this number when the practice becomes more natural for you.

4 Make sure your body stays still and the muscles in your face are relaxed.

5 Practise three rounds of this breathing with an interval of normal breathing between each round.

Bhastrika (breath of fire)

This breath is good for Kapha types in late winter and spring as it increases the vital capacity of the lungs and relieves symptoms of asthma and allergies. It also produces a lovely feeling of heat deep within the body. The in and out breaths are quick and forceful like the function of a pair of bellows used to stoke a fire.

1 Sit comfortably, either cross-legged or on a chair with your feet flat on the floor, but make sure you keep your spine is straight. Rest your hands on your knees, palms facing upwards with your thumb and forefinger touching.
2 Inhale passively and deeply through your nose, allowing your stomach to relax.
3 Then exhale actively with a little force, pulling in your upper abdomen as you do so.
4 Start this pattern of breathing slowly and gradually increase the speed.
5 Do one round of 30 breaths, rest for a minute before repeating the process four to five times.

Caution

Bhastrika is an extremely powerful method of breathing. If it is not practised properly a person can hyperventilate, so find a good yoga teacher who can guide you through the process if you are interested in perfecting this breath.

Ujjayi (breath of victory)

This breath suits all constitutional types and helps to restore your natural state of balance while promoting a sense of strength and victory!

1 Choose a comfortable sitting position, or you might like to practise this lying down, with your arms and legs slightly spread out in the corpse position as illustrated in the previous chapter. Select whichever posture works best for you.
2 Breathe in deeply through your nostrils contracting the muscles at the top of your windpipe – you should hear a light rasping sound at the back of your throat as the you do this.
3 Hold your breath in your belly for a moment, then slowly breathe out, again contracting the muscles at the top of your windpipe so you make a slight hissing sound.
4 Repeat the process for five to ten minutes and then take a few moments to become aware of the deep feelings of joy and contentment this method of breathing can produce.

Some simple meditation practices

Meditation is a journey that cannot be accurately described. To understand its power you have to experience it!

When we achieve a meditative state our breathing slows, our mind stops and we enjoy a sense of effortless self-awareness that allows us to explore and experience our innermost consciousness. This often results in tremendous insights into how we can transform our lives and way of being.

There are many ways to meditate. You may choose to focus on a particular colour or object, recite a personal mantra or simply tune into the rhythm of your natural breath. The simple practices given here will help you to get started; however, it is always best to learn meditation with the help of a good teacher who can guide you through the process and reassure you about your methods of practice. Many courses are available, through your local yoga teacher for example.

The first two exercises given here use the rhythm of your breath to deliver a tranquil state of being and can be done wherever you are in the world. All you need is a quiet place to practise. Alternatively, you might like to use the elements of nature – such as the sky, sea, clouds or a candle flame – as your passport to a deep, meditative state. If this is the first time you have tried meditation you might find focusing on physical objects such as these an easier way to get started.

To get the most from your meditation, practise at a regular time each day. Find a quiet spot and make sure all possible distractions are removed. Unplug the landline and turn off your mobile phone! Don't push yourself too hard at first. Start with just a few minutes of practice and gradually build up to 15–20 minutes a day. Don't worry if you find it hard at first, just keep up your routine and it will come naturally with time. Meditation is a gradual process, so sustained effort is the only way to reach this state. It usually takes about a month of daily practice before any benefits are felt.

Empty bowl meditation

1 Ideally sit cross-legged, in the lotus or half lotus position, or in a chair with your feet flat on the ground. Either way, make sure your spine is straight and rest your hands on your knees, palms facing upwards and open, like empty bowls. If you are not comfortable in a sitting position, you can do this exercise

lying down with your arms and legs slightly apart and palms facing up and open as before.

2 Place your tongue on the roof of your mouth, just behind your teeth, and let your mouth fall slightly open.

3 Start to breathe, slowly and steadily through your nose and, as you do so, focus on the path of your breath. Feel the cool air entering your nostrils on the inhalation and follow this sensation as the air passes down your throat, through the lungs until it reaches the belly button.

4 Now hold your breath for a second or two.

5 Then follow the path of the your exhalation back up the body and out through your nostrils until you can imagine it is lingering about 9 inches in front of your face.

6 Again, hold your breath for a second before repeating the process.

7 Ideally practise this meditation for 15–20 minutes, morning and evening.

So-Hum meditation

So-Hum is actually the sound of our natural breath. The 'so' sound is made when we inhale and the 'hum' sound when we exhale, so this exercise is simply a way of consciously tuning into your natural breath.

1 Sit or lie down as before, whichever is most comfortable for you.

2 Become aware of your natural breath and, in your head, repeat the sound 'so' to yourself on the inhalation and 'hum' on the exhalation.

3 Let your breathing settle into its own rhythm and continue to mentally repeat 'so' and 'hum' to yourself on the inhalation and exhalation for 15–20 minutes.

It may help you to think of 'so' – the inhalation breath – as the life force that cleanses and nourishes our minds and bodies and 'hum' – the exhalation – as a technique we can use to let go of our ego or sense of self.

Meditating on the elements of nature

The next few exercises are all types of Dharana, the branch of yogic meditation where we focus our attention on an object or image. The beauty of these methods is that they use the natural world around us to deliver a deep, meditative state.

Meditating on the sky

Find a quiet space outdoors where you have a clear view of the sky. Lie on your back and gaze into the sky for at least 20 minutes, taking care to avoid looking into the sun if it is out! Notice how cleansed and invigorated your mind feels at the end of this practice. A variation on this exercise is to begin your practice at dusk on a clear evening and meditate on the sky as the stars come out.

Meditating on the clouds

This is a good exercise to practise when there is a contrast of light and dark clouds in the sky. Again, simply lie on your back and focus your full attention on the movement of those clouds as they flit across the sky. Let your thoughts float away with the movement of the clouds.

Meditating on a candle flame

Simply light a candle and gaze into the flame for 15 minutes, trying not to blink. Your eyes will water, but only blink when you absolutely have to. Offer any negative thoughts up to the flame for purification and watch them dissolve away in the flickering light.

Meditating on a water scene

Find a tranquil spot beside the sea, a lake or any stretch of water where you can sit undisturbed. Gaze into the water, letting your thoughts ebb and flow with the motion of the waves. Notice how cool and refreshed you feel at the end of this practice.

Meditating on a mountain

Sit at the brow of a hill or mountain top where you have an uninterrupted view over a valley and other hilltops if possible. Feel grounded and stable like the mountain. Focus on the distant hills and valleys and feel as close as you can to the elements of nature around you.

Using mantras to meditate

Mantra – the repetition of a sacred sound, meaningful word or phrase – promotes a meditative state and has a profound effect on our psychological wellbeing when used correctly. Just think how much our minds are influenced by what we hear, the spoken word or a piece of beautiful music for instance.

The word 'mantra' actually means: 'that which saves the mind'. Just as we use food substances and herbs to treat our bodies, so we can use sound therapeutically to strengthen and heal our minds. Any word or phrase we repeat or memorize is a mantra.

The mind needs positive forms of exercise just like our bodies. Mantra works by changing the energetic structure of our mind to dissolve problems, and it prepares the way to meditation by promoting a sense of focus and a peaceful mental state.

To be effective you need to repeat your chosen mantra 108 times a day for one month, making sure that you pronounce it correctly! You may find it helpful to seek personal instruction from an Ayurvedic practitioner or yoga teacher to ensure the correct pronunciation. If you have high levels of Vata, chant a few times out loud and then continue to repeat your chosen mantra silently in your head. Below are some simple, but extremely powerful, traditional Sanskrit mantras which you might find useful.

- Om (pronounced 'aum' with a resonating 'm' sound) helps to clear the mind, is empowering and builds immunity. It does this by converting Rajasic and Tamasic states of mind to Sattva.
- Ram (with a long 'a' as in 'rather') calms Vata and so helps to resolve problems such as insomnia, anxiety, fear and nightmares.
- Hrim (pronounced 'hreem') cleanses and purifies; it is a useful adjunct to any detoxification process you may be planning.
- Krim (pronounced 'cream') improves our ability to make positive changes in life.
- Klim (pronounced 'kleem') promotes vitality, particularly sexual vigour, while balancing and grounding the self.

Find a quiet place to practise your chosen mantra and make sure you practise it every day. Your mantra can be a word, a life-changing maxim that is meaningful to you or simply a soothing piece of world music or sacred Indian chant.

Some simple alternatives

If the meditation exercises provided so far don't grab you, practising any one of these simple alternatives for 15–20 minutes a day can work just as well.

- Simply count from 1 to 10 in your head, keeping your attention on each number. If your attention wanders, start again from the beginning. Repeat this sequence and notice how calm and clear your mind feels at the end of this practice.

- Use the yoga postures given in the previous chapter as a method of meditation. By stilling the mind, these postures are a potent form of meditation in themselves. Notice how calm and clear your mind feels after your practice.

- Meditate on a colour that appeals to you. In summer you may be drawn to cooling tones of white, silver or green; in winter try warmer shades of red, gold and orange. As with mantras, you need to be consistent and meditate on the same colour for at least a month to reap the rewards.

09

healing herbs, spices and formulations

In this chapter you will learn:
- about the healing herbs and spices in your kitchen cupboard
- therapeutic uses of common Ayurvedic herbal medicines.

Natural medicines for everyday complaints

In this chapter you will learn how to harness the therapeutic effects of a host of healing herbs and spices. You can use this knowledge in your cooking and choice of herbal teas, as well as to give you an insight into any natural remedies you may want to try or be prescribed by an Ayurvedic practitioner.

Ayurveda uses a very wide range of herbs, spices, minerals and metals as medicines. Its pharmacopoeia is one of the largest in the world with some 1,250 substances traditionally in use. While only a fraction of these are currently available outside India, those herbs and spices we do have access to have been used safely and effectively for thousands of years to treat health problems that are still common in the world today, such as insomnia, depression, symptoms of the menopause and obesity.

You may be surprised to learn that many healing Ayurvedic herbs are already lurking in your kitchen cupboard. Common spices such as turmeric, cumin and coriander, for example, have many therapeutic uses, as you will see.

Other lesser-known Ayurvedic herbs, such as Shatavari (Asparagus racemosus) and Gotu Kola (Centella asiatica), are now widely available over the internet and from good health food shops, as well as through Ayurvedic practitioners. At the end of this book you will find details of recommended suppliers of Ayurvedic remedies, as well as industry associations you can contact to find an accredited Ayurvedic doctor or practitioner close to home. As a general rule, it is always best to consult a trained professional before taking any medicines.

Ayurvedic medicines are selected and applied on the same basis as food, that is, by their initial taste, hot or cold potency, post digestive impact, key qualities and the subsequent effect these properties have on the three doshas. For each substance mentioned in this chapter you will find a list of its key properties, doshic effects and therapeutic uses so you can begin to understand a little better how these healing herbs actually work according to Ayurvedic principles. The English, Sanskrit and Latin names for each herb or spice have also been given to help you identify them more easily.

Always choose sustainably grown Ayurvedic herbs

As a consumer of Ayurvedic products, it is incredibly important for you to seek out herbal remedies that have been grown using sustainable methods of farming. This is because the global boom in herbal medicines, and the fact that many herbs are still being harvested from the wild, is putting many plants under the threat of extinction. The World Wildlife Fund estimates that around 20 per cent of the 50,000 or so herbs now used as medicines are at risk. This is especially true of Ayurvedic herbs. To safeguard the future of these healing plants, as well as our environment, make sure you look out for herbal remedies that are sustainably grown and ethically produced.

Healing herbs from your kitchen cupboard

Many kitchen herbs and spices can be used to heal everyday health problems. Once you know more about the impact they have on your mind and body, you can start to use them wisely to treat minor ailments, improve your digestion and overall health.

Asafoetida (Hingu, Ferula foetida)

Rasa (initial taste)	Pungent
Virya (thermal potency)	Heating
Vipaka (post-digestive taste)	Pungent
Gunas (qualities)	Light, oily, penetrating, liquid
Doshic effect	Pacifies Vata and Kapha dosha due to heating effect; aggravates Pitta due to fast-acting and heating properties
Typical uses	Digestive aid, used to cleanse the channels of the body

This Indian plant is the best natural digestive aid and is now commonly found on supermarket shelves. It is particularly useful for reducing the gas-producing effects of most pulses. Add a pinch of asafoetida whenever you cook lentils or mung beans, for example. Asafoetida can also be used to relieve coughs and the symptoms of asthma because of its channel-clearing properties.

Black pepper (Maricha, Piper nigrum)

Rasa	Pungent
Virya	Heating
Vipaka	Pungent
Gunas	Light, penetrating
Doshic effect	Pacifies Kapha and Vata, increases Pitta
Typical uses	Cleanses the GI tract of undigested toxins, analgesic, anti-inflammatory, useful in skin disorders and fever

Black pepper is cleansing and stimulating, making it a great natural remedy for loss of appetite and a good digestive aid. Because it digests fat and speeds up the metabolism it is a useful part of any weight-loss programme. Black pepper stimulates the liver, clears congestion in the lungs and channels of the body and is a powerful nervine tonic.

You can use it as a daily tonic provided you are not Pitta predominant or suffering from a Pitta aggravation. Simply grind seven peppercorns into a fine powder, mix this with a teaspoon of honey and allow it to dissolve on your tongue. The same formula helps to fight the first signs of cold, flu and fever. When a third of a teaspoon of ghee is added to this mixture it increases sexual stamina.

Black pepper powder mixed with a little oil and topically applied is good for chronic skin conditions, such as pruritis, urticaria and leucoderma, as well as newly formed boils, styes and abcesses. Gargling with a little ground black pepper helps to relieve sore throats because of its anti-inflammatory properties.

Cardamom (Ela, Elettaria cardamomum)

Rasa	Pungent
Virya	Cooling
Vipaka	Pungent
Gunas	Light, rough
Doshic effect	Balances all three doshas
Typical uses	Pain relief, skin problems and wound healing, appetizer and digestive aid

Externally cardamom relieves toothache. Simply grind some fresh seeds into a powder and rub it into the affected area. Taken internally it is a good digestive aid, appetizer and mild laxative. Chewing a few seeds after eating, for example, will boost your digestion. It is also an expectorant so can be used to treat coughs, asthma and other respiratory disorders such as bronchitis. Drinking cardamom tea eases stomach ache and travel sickness. When mixed with milk it counteracts the mucus-producing effect of this dairy food and promotes a good night's sleep. Chewing on a few cardomom seeds is also a handy, natural way to quell nicotine cravings if you are giving up smoking! Use it with caution if you suffer from ulcers and other symptoms of aggravated Pitta dosha.

Cinnamon (Twak, Cinnamonum zeylanica)

Rasa	Pungent, bitter, sweet
Virya	Heating
Vipaka	Pungent
Gunas	Light, dry, penetrating
Doshic effect	Pacifies Kapha and Vata, increases Pitta
Typical uses	Blood purifier, liver cleanser, analgesic and deodorant

Used as a mouthwash it combats bad breath and helps to keep the teeth healthy. Chewing cinnamon sticks relieves toothache and nausea. Applied locally it soothes headaches and inflammations. Cinnamon is also appetizing, stimulates the liver and purifies the blood so is a great herbal tea to get into the habit of drinking regularly as well as being a delicious spice to cook with. It is also rich in antiviral, antifungal and antibiotic properties.

Cloves (Lavanga, Syzygium aromaticum)

Rasa	Pungent
Virya	Cooling
Vipaka	Pungent
Gunas	Light, penetrating, oily
Doshic effect	Pacifies Kapha and Pitta dosha
Typical uses	Analgesic, blood disorders, expectorant, fever and skin disorders, aphrodisiac

This is a terrific natural remedy for dental health and pain relief. Clove oil relieves toothache, combats gum disease and bad breath. Use it as a massage oil to relieve the pain caused by rheumatism, sciatica and backache generally. Local application also soothes headaches and sinusitis. Taken internally it stimulates the circulation, strengthens the heart and cleanses the channels of the body, particularly the lymphatic system, making it a useful treatment for colds, coughs, asthma, bronchitis and other forms of lung congestion. Cloves are a powerful aphrodisiac and promote the production of breast milk. The powder of cloves mixed with a little honey is also a safe and natural way to relieve morning sickness.

Coriander/Cilantro (Dhanyaka, Coriandrum sativum)

Rasa	Astringent, bitter, sweet
Virya	Cooling (leaves), slightly heating (seeds)
Vipaka	Sweet
Gunas	Light, oily
Doshic effect	Balances all three doshas; coriander leaves, being cold in potency, are particularly effective in soothing Pitta dosha
Typical uses	Analgesic, anti-inflammatory, relieves internal heat/burning sensations/thirst, colic, digestive aid and liver stimulant

The highly cooling leaves of the coriander plant actually balance all three doshas and are used to treat a wide variety of diseases. Being sweet, bitter and astringent coriander is particularly good for relieving high levels of Pitta dosha. You can use both the seeds and leaves, but be aware that the seeds are more heating. It is good for treating fevers, quenching thirst and is the best natural diuretic. Taken as an infusion it eases stomach ache, indigestion, diarrhoea, nausea and urinary tract problems such as cystitis. Made into a paste or infusion, coriander leaves can be used externally to treat conjunctivitis and headaches.

Cumin (Jeerak, Cuminum cyminum)

Rasa	Pungent
Virya	Heating
Vipaka	Pungent
Gunas	Light, dry
Doshic effect	Pacifies Vata and Kapha but increases Pitta due to its heating effect
Typical uses	Digestive aid, blood purifier, skin conditions, oedema (swelling)

Like its sister spices fennel and dill, cumin is a good digestive spice being both appetizing and carminative. Cooking with cumin, or simply chewing the seeds after a meal, aids digestion as well as relieving indigestion, gas and bloating. It is particularly useful if you eat a lot of wheat as it helps to break down this hard-to-digest grain. Cumin is a diuretic so relieves symptoms of oedema and water retention when taken internally or applied locally as a paste to the affected area. It is also blood purifying and extremely good for the skin so, if you suffer from any kind of skin problem, make cumin a regular part of your diet.

Dill (Mishreya, Anethum sowa)

Rasa	Pungent, bitter
Virya	Heating
Vipaka	Pungent
Gunas	Light, dry, penetrating
Doshic effect	Useful in disorders caused by Vata and Kapha dosha
Typical uses	Colic, digestive aid, problem periods

A member of the fennel family, dill has a powerful antispasmodic effect, which is why it is the key ingredient of gripe water. Use it to relieve stomach cramps and diarrhoea, particularly in children. It is also good for easing period pains. Like cumin and fennel, it stimulates digestion, is diuretic so helps relieve oedema and water retention and is useful in skin disorders.

Fennel (Shatapushpa, Foeniculum vulgare)

Rasa	Sweet, pungent, bitter
Virya	Neutral
Vipaka	Pungent or sweet depending on variety
Gunas	Light, oily
Doshic effect	Pacifies Vata, Pitta and Kapha dosha
Typical uses	Brain tonic, digestive aid and laxative, blood and menstrual disorders, colic

You often see people in India chewing fennel seeds after they eat. That's because it is a powerful digestive, gentle laxative and diuretic, so helps to cleanse the digestive tract of unwanted toxins. Like dill and cumin it eases stomach cramps and is useful for relieving period pains and regulating the menstrual cycle. Try frying fennel seeds with a little fresh ginger root or boiling it in milk to relieve stomach ache in children. If you are pregnant, including fennel in your diet can help to relieve morning sickness. If you are a nursing mother, it will improve the flow of your breast milk. Fennel is also considered the most Sattvic (see glossary) spice, because of its sweet taste and neutral potency, making it a useful brain tonic.

Fenugreek (Methika, Trigonella foenicum-graecum)

Rasa	Pungent, bitter
Virya	Heating
Vipaka	Pungent
Doshic effect	Useful in Vata and Kapha disorders, increases Pitta
Typical uses	Rejuvenator, loss of appetite, post natal aid, abdominal pain

This is one of the most useful herbs to cook with if you have too much Vata in your system or simply can't give up Vata-increasing foods! It is also a rejuvenating tonic used in Ayurveda to promote longevity, soothe troubled nerves and reduce the impact of degenerative diseases such as rheumatoid arthritis. Don't use it if you are pregnant but, after giving birth, it helps to promote breast milk production and normalize the menstrual cycle. Avoid fenugreek if you are strongly Pitta predominant or are currently suffering from high levels of Pitta dosha.

Garlic (Rasona, Allium sativum)

Rasa	Sweet, salty, pungent, bitter, astringent
Virya	Heating
Vipaka	Pungent
Gunas	Oily, penetrating, slimy, heavy, liquid
Doshic effect	Pacifies Kapha and Vata dosha
Typical uses	Rejuvenator, analgesic, aphrodisiac, brain and heart tonic

Widely considered to be a panacea for a multitude of ailments, garlic has many therapeutic effects but, like any potent medicine, should be used wisely. Taken too frequently it is Tamasic (see glossary) and so slows down the mental functions. Garlic is particularly useful if you have a heart condition because it lowers LDL cholesterol and triglycerides as well as reducing blood clotting, so helping to minimize the risk of heart attacks and strokes. It promotes a healthy metabolism, stimulates the immune system and cleanses the channels of the body, so helping to prevent artherosclerosis. Made into a paste and applied topically, garlic is pain relieving and anti-inflammatory so can be used to treat rheumatoid arthritis and sciatica. Avoid garlic if you are pregnant, if you suffer from hyperacidity or other symptoms of excess Pitta.

Fresh ginger (Ardraka, Zingiber officinalis)

Rasa	Pungent, sweet
Virya	Heating
Vipaka	Pungent (dry variety is sweet)
Gunas	Dry, penetrating, heavy
Doshic effect	Pacifies Vata and Pitta dosha, increases Pitta
Typical uses	Excellent appetizer and digestive aid, analgesic, antiemetic, aphrodisiac, carminative, nervine tonic, expectorant, useful in rheumatoid arthritis

Fresh ginger root is a powerful natural remedy for reducing excess levels of Vata, stimulating the digestion and eliminating ama (undigested toxins). Get into the habit of drinking a cup of fresh ginger root tea after your meals. It is also a good way to stimulate the appetite of children who are fussy or poor eaters. To make it more palatable for them, try juicing a centimetre or so of fresh ginger root together with some fresh apples or oranges. A slice of fresh ginger marinated with lemon juice and sprinkled with a little rock salt is also a good way to kickstart your digestive enzymes before a meal. Being stimulating, warming and analgesic in nature, ginger is good for rheumatism, common colds, fevers, sore throats, menstrual cramps and can be used to relieve morning sickness, travel sickness and even vertigo!

Nutmeg (Jatiphala, Myristica fragrans)

Rasa	Pungent, bitter, astringent
Virya	Heating
Vipaka	Pungent
Gunas	Light, oily, penetrating
Doshic effect	Useful in relieving Vata and Kapha disorders
Typical uses	Analgesic, aphrodisiac, insomnia, impotency due to premature ejaculation, dysmenorrhoea

Nutmeg balances Vata and Kapha due to its hot, bitter and pungent qualities and is the best sedative of all the spices. Use it sparingly for best results. A pinch of nutmeg in a cup of hot milk helps insomnia and anxiety. In low doses it also stimulates the circulation, is an aphrodisiac and useful remedy for sexual health problems such as impotency and premature ejaculation. Use it when fever and diarrhoea occur simultaneously and as a tonic for post-diarrhoeal weakness. Made into a paste and applied topically it is pain relieving and a natural deodorant. Mixed with water and dry ginger powder it relieves headaches caused by the common cold.

Turmeric root (Haridra, Curcuma longa)

Rasa	Bitter, pungent
Virya	Heating
Vipaka	Pungent
Gunas	Dry, light
Doshic effect	Pacifies Kapha and Vata
Typical uses	Anti-inflammatory, wound healer, analgesic, useful in joint disorders and skin disorders

Fresh turmeric root is one of nature's most powerful anti-inflammatory agents, a potent blood purifier and natural wound healer. In clinical studies it has been shown to reduce the levels of arachidonic acid in the body which cause inflammation. This makes it useful for rheumatoid and osteoarthritis, as well as a host of stubborn skin conditions including dermatitis, eczema, urticaria and psoriasis. By increasing the blood flow through the hepatic system, turmeric purifies the blood and is often used to clear systemic toxaemia and beautify the skin. Its Sanskrit name actually means: 'that which improves the skin'. It is also great for healing wounds and diabetic boils. Simply mix it with a little honey and apply to the affected area. Use it in your cooking or steep it in a cup of hot water to make a spicy infusion. Avoid turmeric if you are pregnant or on anticoagulant medication.

Common herbal remedies

In this section you will learn more about some of the more specialized single herbs Ayurveda has to offer. The herbs mentioned here are widely available, safe and effective but – for best results – it is always advisable to consult a trained professional before use.

Amalaki (Indian Gooseberry, Emblica officinalis)

Rasa	Sweet, sour, bitter, pungent, astringent
Virya	Cooling
Vipaka	Sweet
Gunas	Light, dry
Doshic effect	Balances all three doshas
Typical uses	Rejuvenator, aphrodisiac, brain and heart tonic, skin disorders

The supreme, rejuvenating herb and Indian equivalent to ginseng, this nourishing, revitalizing fruit balances all three doshas and is a key ingredient in many popular Ayurvedic formulations, including Triphala and Chyawanaprash, as well as being available as a single herb. With 20 times as much vitamin C as your average lemon, Amalaki is a potent immunity tonic and natural heart healer. It has long-lasting antioxidant effects, liver cleansing properties and protects the heart by reducing LDL cholesterol and healing arterial damage.

Arjuna (Arjuna Myrolaban, Terminalia arjuna)

Rasa	Astringent
Virya	Cooling
Vipaka	Pungent
Gunas	Light, dry
Doshic effect	Pacifies Kapha and Pitta doshas
Typical uses	Heart tonic, oedema (swelling)

The leaves and root bark of the Arjuna tree are cooling and astringent, so used to treat Kapha- and Pitta-related problems. It is the best herb in the Ayurvedic pharmacopoeia for heart complaints and is used to improve the rhythm and function of the heart, increase blood pressure and treat angina. It is also useful for treating coughs and the symptoms of tuberculosis.

Ashwagandha (Winter Cherry, Withania somnifera)

Rasa	Sweet
Virya	Heating
Vipaka	Sweet, astringent, bitter
Gunas	Heavy, oily, slimy
Doshic effect	Pacifies Vata and Kapha dosha
Typical uses	Nervine tonic, aphrodisiac, rejuvenator, useful in rheumatoid arthritis and other degenerative conditions

A potent remedy for many health problems caused by the frenetic pace of modern living, Ashwagandha is a rejuvenating herb said to give you the strength of a horse and have powerful anti-ageing properties! It works by nourishing the nervous system and building immunity. Useful in all forms of stress-related disorders, particularly insomnia and anxiety, this herb is also a natural aphrodisiac that promotes semen production and strengthens the uterus. Recent clinical studies have found that Ashwagandha actually slows the ageing process by building haemoglobin and strengthening the tissues of the body while reducing levels of serum cholesterol.

Brahmi (Herpestis monnieri)

Rasa	Bitter, astringent
Virya	Cooling
Vipaka	Pungent
Gunas	Light, slightly oily
Doshic effect	Balances all three doshas
Typical uses	Brain tonic, rejuvenator, useful in depression

This cold, bitter-tasting herb is to be found in many Ayurvedic remedies because it nourishes all the tissues of the body, especially the brain and nervous system. It is used to treat depression as well as forms of mania and epilepsy. In small doses it has cardiotonic properties and increases the blood pressure.

Gotu kola (Indian Pennywort, Centella asiatica)

Rasa	Bitter, astringent
Virya	Cooling
Vipaka	Sweet
Gunas	Dry, light
Doshic effect	Balances all three doshas, especially Kapha and Vata
Typical uses	Brain tonic, nervine tonic, analgesic, antipyretic, antispasmodic, anti-inflammatory

Famous for its mind-enhancing properties, the leaves of this herb even look like the cerebellum! Gotu kola leaf is a favourite with the student fraternity because of its ability to improve concentration, memory and alertness. It is useful in Alzheimer's, senility and general ageing as well as all forms of stress and emotional upset. Its moisturizing and stimulating effect on the circulation also makes it a terrific natural remedy for cellulite and varicose veins.

Guduchi (Tinospora cordifolia)

Rasa	Bitter, astringent
Virya	Heating
Vipaka	Sweet
Gunas	Light, oily
Doshic effect	Balances all three doshas, especially Vata and Pitta
Typical uses	Appetizer, rejuvenator, blood purifier, detoxifier

In Sanskrit its name means: 'one which protects the body'. Guduchi cleans the system of inflammatory toxins and eliminates uric acid via the urine, making it a useful remedy for gout, pain in the joints and inflammatory arthritis as well as diabetes. Its powerful cleansing properties are used to treat stubborn skin conditions such as psoriasis, eczema, acne and boils as well as liver disorders. It also has a rasayana effect and is often used by Ayurvedic physicians to build tissues and strength in people suffering from cancer and arthritis.

Guggulu (Indian Myrrh, Commiphora mukul)

Rasa	Bitter, pungent, astringent, sweet
Virya	Heating
Vipaka	Pungent
Gunas	Light, penetrating, dry
Doshic effect	Balances all three doshas but can aggravate Pitta if used to excess due to its hot, pungent qualities
Typical uses	Clears fat tissue, blood purifier, rejuvenator, stimulates digestive fire, useful for weight loss and managing cholesterol problems

This plant resin actually scrapes lipids and cholesterol residues from the channels of the body, making it an effective remedy for high cholesterol levels, heart conditions and obesity. Guggulu has a specific action in reducing inflammation in arthritis and has been found to heal acne. It is often used to intensify the therapeutic effect of other detoxifying herbal remedies such as Triphala and Trikatu.

Haritaki (Chebulic myrobalans, Terminalia chebula)

Rasa	Astringent, bitter, pungent, sweet, sour
Virya	Heating
Vipaka	Sweet
Gunas	Light, dry
Doshic effect	Balances all three doshas
Typical uses	Nervine tonic, laxative, rejuvenator

This versatile fruit is a key ingredient of Triphala – the Ayurvedic 'three fruits' formulation – and a powerful natural laxative that balances all three doshas, making it an effective rejuvenator. It can be taken throughout the year as a rasayana with:

- a little salt in wet weather
- honey in spring
- treacle in summer
- unrefined sugar in autumn/fall
- ginger in winter.

Its laxative action makes it useful in constipation while its antipyretic and anti-inflammatory properties mean it is also effective in treating chronic fever and piles.

Kumari (Aloe vera)

Rasa	Bitter, sweet
Virya	Cooling
Vipaka	Pungent
Gunas	Oily, slimy
Doshic effect	Balances all three doshas, particularly Pitta dosha due to its cold, bitter, sweet qualities
Typical uses	Rejuvenator, useful in colic, skin inflammations and burns, dysentery, conjunctivitis

The juice made from the leaves of the aloe vera plant is a refrigerant making it useful in complaints arising from high levels of Pitta such as heartburn, hypertension, migraine and period pains. It is also commonly used to treat skin conditions such as psoriasis and to soothe sunburn.

Meshashringi (Gymnema sylvestra)

Rasa	Astringent
Virya	Heating
Vipaka	Pungent
Gunas	Light, dry
Doshic effect	Relieves Kapha and Vata dosha
Typical uses	Diabetes

This incredible herb is a unique treatment for all types of diabetes and can be taken safely with insulin or as a natural alternative to oral anti-hyperglycaemic agents. Not only does it lower blood sugar levels by increasing insulin production, it actually blocks our ability to taste 'sweet' foods, so helping people to avoid the sweet, sugary foods that are known to trigger type 2 diabetes.

Neem (Margosa tree, Azadirachta indica)

Rasa	Bitter
Virya	Cooling
Vipaka	Pungent
Gunas	Light, dry
Doshic effect	Reduces Pitta and Kapha, increases Vata
Typical uses	Inflammatory skin conditions, inflammatory intestinal problems such as colitis, diabetes, high fever

A renowned antibacterial herb, Neem is extremely bitter making it one of the best detoxifying herbs in the Ayurvedic pharmacopaeia. It is a superb remedy for liver, skin and digestive problems and a key ingredient of many Ayurvedic remedies for the skin, hair and nails. It can be used to regulate intestinal flora by eliminating bad bacteria from the GI tract and to treat fungal infections such as candida. Its anti-inflammatory effect makes it useful for stomach ulcers, ulcerative colitis and Crohn's disease. More recently it has been found to help prevent the onset of type 2 diabetes and lower blood sugar levels if diabetes does occur. Being a detoxifier, Neem should not be used in pregnancy or when there is weakness with wasting and debility.

Punanarva (Spreading hogweed, Boerhavia diffusa)

Rasa	Pungent, bitter, astringent, sweet
Virya	Cooling
Vipaka	Pungent
Doshic effect	Balances all three doshas
Typical uses	Rejuvenator, diuretic so useful in oedema, cardiac tonic, asthma

This is a particularly good rasayana for Kapha types because of its natural affinity for the heart and respiratory tract. Taken regularly, Punanarva protects from and treats many Kapha-related conditions including heart disease, oedema, persistent coughs and asthma. It also tones up the kidneys and is therefore an excellent natural remedy for urinary disorders and other kidney-related problems.

Shatavari (Wild asparagus, Asparagus racemosus)

Rasa	Bitter, sweet
Virya	Cooling
Vipaka	Sweet
Gunas	Oily, heavy
Doshic effect	Reduces Vata and Pitta, increases Kapha
Typical uses	Rejuvenator, female reproductive tonic, aphrodisiac

Shatavari is the supreme women's tonic used for thousands of years to treat a broad range of female sexual health problems because of its natural affinity for the female reproductive organs. Its name actually means: 'she who has a hundred husbands'! Not only does Shatavari promote fertility, regulate erratic menstrual cycles and increase breast milk production, it is also the natural alternative to HRT used to treat symptoms of the menopause such as hot flushes, night sweats, irritability, erratic memory, dryness and weight gain safely and effectively. It is actually useful for both sexes. In men, Shatavari increases the sperm count.

Yastimadhu (Licorice, Glycerrhiza glabra)

Rasa	Sweet
Virya	Cooling
Vipaka	Sweet
Gunas	Heavy, oily
Doshic effect	Pacifies Vata and Pitta
Typical uses	Rejuvenator, nervous disorders, laryngitis, coughs and colds, aphrodisiac

This is a powerful rejuvenator for Vata and Pitta types and a terrific natural remedy for sore throats, strained vocal chords and the common cold. Licorice is soothing, nourishing and promotes the memory. If you can get your hands on licorice root you can either chew it or infuse it in a cup of hot water and take it as a tea. When mixed with unequal quantities of ghee, honey and milk it is a powerful aphrodisiac that also increases sperm count. Taken with honey it is good for relieving coughs and the symptoms of asthma.

Authentic Ayurvedic formulations

Most good suppliers of Ayurvedic medicines include the following formulations in their repertoire of natural remedies. The advantage of compound formulations is that the various ingredients work together to intensify the overall therapeutic effect and reduce or eliminate any potential side effects a single ingredient could have if taken in isolation.

Avipathika churna (powder) to cleanse the GI tract

This is the formulation of choice for Pitta imbalances. Its principle ingredient is the Indian herb Trivrut (Operculina turpethum) which, through its mild purgative action, gently removes excessive levels of Pitta from the GI tract. A variety of other digestive and laxative herbs and spices such as ginger, black pepper, cardamom, amalaki and haritaki are included in this formulation to increase its overall effect. Avipathika churna (powder) is used whenever the digestive fire is low and to relieve Pitta-related conditions such as heartburn, hyperacidity, burning sensations and abdominal pain. It should be taken with some warm water.

Chyawanaprash for daily rejuvenation

This rejuvenating elixir of 40 different fruits, spices, herbs and honey is made from an ancient recipe which has been used for thousands of years. It boosts the body's natural resistance to infectious diseases by building haemoglobin and white blood cells. It is particularly good for people who get repeated coughs and colds as it nourishes the mucus membranes and helps to clear phlegm. It is also good for low libido and fertility problems, for strengthening the mind and body after a prolonged illness or simply as a general immunity tonic. Take one to two teaspoons daily to build strength, energy and stamina. It is delicious on its own and its therapeutic properties are enhanced when it is taken with a glass of warm milk.

Dashamoola kwath (decoction) for pain relief

This multipurpose combination of ten herb roots is renowned for its pain-relieving properties. It is mainly used to treat Vata and Kapha disorders and is a powerful anti-inflammatory and analgesic. Its ama-digesting capabilities make it a useful remedy for asthma, fever and oedema and it is also widely used to treat conditions associated with pain such as sciatica, arthritis, gout and all forms of backache. Its ability to relieve tremors makes it especially useful in treating Parkinson's disease.

Hingvastaka churna (powder) for stimulating digestive fire

The key ingredient in this formulation is hingu, otherwise known as asafoetida, a common kitchen spice. This powerful compound formulation also includes ginger, cumin and black pepper. It is the remedy of choice for stimulating the appetite and improving digestion. Use it with caution if you are a Pitta type or have symptoms of a Pitta aggravation as Hinvastaka churna is very hot in potency, so should not be taken for prolonged periods of time in this instance.

Sitopaladi churna (powder) for lung complaints

This is the best formulation for digesting excess mucus and a powerful expectorant that rejuvenates the respiratory system. It is traditionally taken with honey and ghee to treat bronchial asthma, chronic bronchitis and fever.

Trikatu for head colds, allergies and sluggish digestion

A combination of three hot spices – black pepper, ginger and pippali – Trikatu stimulates sluggish digestion and digests ama (undigested toxins). It has a natural affinity for the lungs and orifices of the head making it a superb treatment for winter colds as it clears mucus, coughs and breathing difficulties as well as treating the symptoms of asthma, bronchitis and allergic rhinitis. It also speeds up the metabolism, helping to reduce LDL cholesterol. Use with caution if you have high levels of Pitta or are pregnant as Trikatu may be too spicy for you!

Triphala for constipation and weight loss

Triphala is a blend of three Indian fruits – haritaki, amalaki and bibhitaki – used to purify the intestines and nourish the tissues of the body. A mild laxative, one of its benefits is that – unlike many other remedies for constipation – it is safe for long-term use. It is traditionally used to maintain a healthy digestive tract, cleanse and strengthen the lungs so is useful if you suffer from allergic rhinitis, hayfever or sinusitis. Used as an eyewash Triphala is highly effective in treating eye inflammations such as styes and conjunctivitis. Its balanced spectrum of five tastes has also been found to reduce food cravings and prevent over-eating making it useful as part of any weight loss programme when combined with a sensible diet. Being a laxative, Triphala should not be taken in isolation during pregnancy. It can however be added to other herbal ingredients and used as a general tonic/rejuvenator by pregnant women.

10

self-healing secrets for common complaints

In this chapter you will learn:
- how to treat common complaints with diet, lifestyle practices and some simple home remedies.

Holistic methods of healing

In this chapter we are going to focus on the self-healing steps you can take to treat everyday complaints. Ayurveda has a long history of treating many common health problems, naturally and effectively. Its approach is to use a holistic blend of diet, lifestyle practices and natural remedies.

In deep-rooted and complex conditions such as arthritis and diabetes you would be wise to consult a good Ayurvedic practitioner for best results but, even then, there are some simple things you can do at home to ease the symptoms and improve your overall quality of life.

To make this section as practical as possible, the majority of remedies given use foods, herbs and spices generally found in the kitchen. In those instances where more specialized Ayurvedic herbal remedies are mentioned these can be sourced through the list of suppliers provided in Appendix 2 of this book or via a qualified Ayurvedic practitioner.

Acne

This is a symptom of high levels of Pitta. The first step is to follow the Pitta-pacifying diet given in Chapter 6, making sure you cut out spicy, fermented, salty, fried and citrus foods in particular. Then there are several practices you can build into your day to improve your skin.

Home remedies

- Take 1 tsp of ghee with $\frac{1}{4}$ tsp turmeric powder in the morning on an empty stomach.
- Drink a cup of cumin seed, coriander seed and fennel seed tea after each meal. Simply infuse a $\frac{1}{3}$ tsp of each spice in a cup of hot water for ten minutes before drinking it.
- Make a healing paste from 1 tsp of chickpea flour (found in any Asian supermarket) and a little water. Apply it to the affected area and leave it to dry for 30 minutes before washing it off. Alternatively you can mix a little almond powder with water. Crush some fresh peeled almonds in a pestle and mortar or coffee grinder and apply as before.
- Rub fresh melon onto your skin at bedtime and leave it overnight. Melon is extremely cooling, so pacifies Pitta while healing and softening the skin.

Lifestyle practices

- Build more cooling yoga postures and methods of pranayama into your daily routine, such as the moon salutations (see Chapter 7) and Shitali (cooling breath) given in Chapter 8.
- Avoid exposure to the sun and other forms of external heat.
- Don't pinch your pimples. It spreads infection to other areas and leads to scarring.

Low appetite and agni (digestive fire)

These remedies are useful whenever you suffer from a poor appetite or a sluggish digestion (the typical signs of which are a whitish coating of the tongue, feeling heavy and lethargic especially in the morning and after eating, as well as heavy, strong-smelling stools, often with mucus).

Dietary guidelines

- Follow a light diet of easily digestible foods such as plenty of leafy green vegetables, vegetable and mung-bean soups. Avoid all foods that are hard to digest, particularly processed wheat products, dairy foods, potatoes and tomatoes.
- Use plenty of ghee and digestive spices in your cooking, such as fennel, dry ginger powder, cumin, coriander, garlic, black pepper, asafoetida, caraway seeds, dill seeds, cloves, cinnamon, celery seeds, rock salt, mustard seeds and ajwain seeds. All these ingredients can be found on supermarket shelves or at your local Asian grocery store.
- Drink a cup of hot ginger water after every meal (made with grated fresh root of ginger steeped in hot water for five to ten minutes).

Home remedies

- Slice some fresh ginger root, soak this in lemon juice for a couple of hours and then rub each slice with a little rock salt. Dry them on a radiator and store. Chew one slice for five to ten minutes before food or after your meal.
- Make a tea from $\frac{1}{2}$ tsp cumin powder, $\frac{1}{2}$ tsp of ginger powder, a pinch of asafoetida and 1 pinch of rock salt. Mix the ingredients in $\frac{1}{2}$ a glass of warm water and drink twice daily.

Lifestyle practices

- Practise the Bhastrika (breath of fire) described in Chapter 8, this will help to rekindle your digestive fire.

Anxiety

An increasingly common problem today, anxiety is due to high levels of Vata dosha. Typical symptoms include feelings of fear, shortness of breath, heart palpitations and even panic attacks. There is no magic bullet for healing anxiety; relief comes from building certain practices into your everyday life so that, eventually, they become second nature. There is no doubt, however, that with concerted effort and self-discipline you can get this debilitating condition under control.

Lifestyle practices

- The most important thing you can do is to practise a deep breathing exercise for at least ten minutes every day. Once you've mastered the art of deep breathing you will start to feel much calmer and can use the breath to pacify an attack if it does occur. The reason breathing is so effective is that the typical symptoms of anxiety – light headedness, mental confusion, heart palpitations, numb and tingly limbs – are all due to a lack of oxygen. When we are anxious our breathing becomes shallower. As a result we don't take in the levels of oxygen we need to feed our minds and bodies properly, it's as simple as that. Get into the habit of lying in the corpse position and practising the abdominal breath given in Chapter 7.

Home remedies

- In the morning take 1 tsp of ghee on an empty stomach with a cup of hot water. It helps to relieve tension and nourish the central nervous system.
- You may also find it helpful to apply a little ghee regularly to your temples throughout the day.
- Make yourself an anxiety-beating brew to drink throughout the day. Mix 1 tsp cumin powder, 1 tsp coriander powder, $\frac{1}{2}$ tsp fennel seed powder, 20 rose petals and 1 tsp of raw cane sugar in a cup of hot water. Boil these ingredients for five minutes, remove from the heat and allow to stand for 20 minutes before filtering and drinking the liquid as and when desired.
- If you suffer from heart palpitations, drink a glass of orange juice with 1 tsp of honey and a pinch of nutmeg for instant relief.
- Before going to bed add $\frac{1}{3}$ cup of fresh ginger root and $\frac{1}{3}$ cup of baking soda to a hot bath and relax in it for 10–15 minutes.

- After your bath, give yourself an oil massage using sesame oil if you are a Vata type, coconut oil if you are Pitta and corn oil if you are Kapha.
- Alternatively, get into the habit of rubbing 2 tbsp of sesame oil into the crown of your head just before bed. Protect your pillow with a towel; sleep with the oil on and wash it off in the morning.

Arthritis

Arthritis is a complex and degenerative condition so, for best results, seek the help of a qualified Ayurvedic practitioner. The various forms of arthritis can be due to a Vata, Pitta or Kapha imbalance; however, in every case, a critical factor in the disease is a sluggish digestion, which causes ama (undigested toxins) to build up and block tissue nourishment leading to pain, stiffness and inflammation of the joints. The first step in any treatment, therefore, is to reduce ama and so ease the symptoms of this debilitating condition.

Dietary guidelines

- Eat plenty of warm, fresh, simple home-cooked foods such as vegetable soups and rice dishes seasoned with digestive spices such as garlic, ginger, ajwain, cumin, coriander and asafoetida.
- It is vital to avoid all heavy, cold, oily and mucus-promoting foods, particularly wheat, pork, red meat and dairy products such as milk, yoghurt and ice cream.
- Drink lots of hot water throughout the day and have a cup of freshly made ginger tea after each meal. This will help to flush toxins from the system. Avoid chilled and iced drinks of all kinds.
- Avoid stale, tinned, refrigerated and frozen foods as well as foods containing preservatives. The saying 'fresh is best' really does hold true when aiming to relieve the symptoms of arthritis.
- Eat smaller quantities of food and have your evening meal as early as possible, ideally before 7p.m. to give yourself time to digest it fully before going to bed.

Home remedies

- At bedtime swallow 1 tsp of castor oil and $\frac{1}{3}$ tsp of whole fenugreek seeds and wash them down with another cup of hot ginger water sweetened with $\frac{1}{2}$ tsp of honey. These remedies cleanse the colon and help to scrape ama from the joints.

- To relieve joint pain and inflammation, take $\frac{1}{4}$ kg of dry ginger powder and $\frac{1}{4}$ kg of ajwain powder and tie them up together in a tea-towel to make a bolus. Heat the bolus by holding it very carefully against the surface of a hot iron, and apply it to the affected area for 10–20 minutes in a pounding motion. Keep the hot iron to hand so you can re-heat the bolus as and when required throughout this treatment.

- For rheumatoid arthritis, living on a fasting drink for three days can significantly ease the pain and stiffness. Mix 5 cups of water with 2 tsp of cumin powder, 2 tsp of coriander powder, 20 rose petals, 4 cardamom pods, 1 tsp fennel seed powder, 3 pinches of ajwain powder, $\frac{1}{2}$ tsp of ginger powder and 1 pinch of asafoetida. Simmer the mix for five minutes, remove from heat, cover and let it stand for 20 minutes. Filter and decant it into a thermos flask so you can drink this brew regularly throughout the day. Once you have finished your fast, gradually return to a normal diet, starting off with a simple rice gruel and slowly re-introducing more complex foods over a 14-day period. Refer back to Chapter 4 for more dietary guidelines on the foods to favour immediately after you break your fast.

- For osteoarthritis, soak 1 tbsp of sesame seeds in $\frac{1}{4}$ cup of water for two hours. Blend and filter. Drinking this sesame milk twice a day will help to nourish and strengthen your bone tissue.

Lifestyle practices

- Avoid sleeping during the day as this promotes Kapha and so slows down the processes of digestion and metabolism.
- Protect yourself from cold, damp weather conditions.
- If you suffer from rheumatoid arthritis, avoid the use of massage oils as their unctuous qualities will increase the levels of ama in your system. Instead use the dry, hot bolus method of pain-relieving herbs described to give symptomatic relief.
- Get into the habit of practising yoga as these postures loosen stiff joints, build strength and improve flexibility without putting too much pressure on painful joints. It's best to seek the help of a qualified yoga teacher who can teach you the most therapeutic postures to practise for your condition.

Asthma

This chronic condition is largely a Kapha problem, although Vata is also involved. In the vast majority of cases – around 90 per cent – asthma is due to poor digestion caused by an excess of heavy, indigestible foods such as wheat, milk, yeast, cheese, sweets and fried foods. While pollutants, pollen and dust can also be contributing factors they are usually secondary triggers. The following remedies can be highly effective when they are made a feature of your daily life.

Dietary guidelines

- Eat only light, freshly cooked foods that are easy to digest. Avoid completely all mucus-producing foods such as curds, banana, ice cream, sweets, cold drinks, refined white sugar, peanuts, fried and oily foods as well as potatoes and tomatoes.

- Use plenty of digestive spices in your cooking such as garlic, ginger, onion, coriander, black pepper, mustard and asafoetida.

Home remedies

- Licorice tea is a great home remedy because it has the power to prevent as well as pacify asthma attacks. Once made, it will keep for up to 72 hours without losing its potency, so you can make up a batch and keep it to hand for emergencies or take it throughout the day as a preventative measure. Simply boil a teaspoon of licorice root in a cup of water for five minutes.

Caution

If you suffer from hypertension only take licorice tea in emergencies as regular consumption will increase your sodium levels.

- For long-term prevention, try one of these two remedies:
  - Mix 1 tsp of cinnamon with $\frac{1}{4}$ tsp of Trikatu (see Appendix 2 for suppliers) in a cup of hot water. Let it stand for ten minutes then add 1 tsp of honey. Take this twice daily.
  - Mix $\frac{1}{4}$ cup onion juice with 1 tsp of honey and $\frac{1}{8}$ tsp black pepper and drink.

Lifestyle practices

- Breathing techniques are a really powerful way to prevent and pacify asthma attacks. Any one of the methods of pranayama already described will increase your lung capacity and help to reduce feelings of tightness in the chest and breathlessness. In particular, focus your attention on the 'out breath' or exhalation and make sure you practise your chosen method of breathing daily so it becomes second nature. Then you can switch on your controlled breathing technique whenever you need it to ease the intensity of an attack or overcome it altogether
- Practise therapeutic yoga asanas such as the cobra, shoulder stand and plough, which open up the heart chakra (energy centre) and increase lung capacity.

Panchakarma

- The cleansing therapies of panchakarma described in Chapter 4 can greatly relieve – and sometimes even cure – chronic asthma. If you suffer from chronic or acute attacks seek the help of an Ayurvedic doctor who specializes in the methods of panchakarma.

Bad Breath

This is a sign of poor digestion and is due to a build-up of ama (undigested toxins) in the GI tract. You can tell if there is ama in your system by examining your tongue first thing in the morning, if it has a whitish coating, ama is present!

Dietary guidelines

- Avoid heavy foods that are hard to digest and increase your use of digestive spices such as ginger, black pepper, cumin, coriander and asafoetida.
- After each meal, chew 1 tsp of roasted fennel and cumin seeds and wash it down with a cup of fresh ginger-root tea.

Balding

This is common in Pitta individuals and people with a Pitta aggravation. By reducing the levels of Pitta dosha in the system, hair loss can be significantly reduced.

Dietary guidelines

- Follow the Pitta-pacifying diet described in Chapter 6 making sure you include plenty of cooling, nourishing foods in your diet, such as dairy products (if your digestion is strong enough), cooked apples, fresh coconut, cabbage and sesame seeds.

- Be sure to have enough zinc, calcium and magnesium in your diet. Pumpkin seeds and alfafa sprouts are rich in zinc; quinoa and sesame seeds are excellent sources of calcium; and for magnesium make sure you include a regular dose of pulses and wholegrains. Notice how this benefits not just your hair but also your nails!

Home remedies

- Drink a cup of aloe vera juice three times a day for at least three months.

- Or you may prefer to take the following remedy in the morning on an empty stomach. Take 1 cup of milk, 1 tsp ghee, 1 tsp sesame seeds (soaked overnight) and 4 almonds (soaked overnight and peeled). Blend all the ingredients together, warm this mixture slightly and finally add a little raw cane sugar.

- At bedtime, massage a little coconut oil into your scalp and the soles of your feet and leave it on overnight. You can protect your bed linen by covering your pillow with a towel and wearing a pair of socks to bed!

- Alternatively, combine $\frac{1}{4}$ cup of freshly grated coconut, 4 almonds (soaked overnight and peeled), $\frac{1}{2}$ cup of water and 1 tbsp sesame seeds. Crush all the ingredients together in a coffee grinder or pestle and mortar. Filter well and massage this mixture into the scalp. Again, you need to leave it on overnight and rinse it off in the morning.

Specialist Ayurvedic therapies

- Indian head treatment, otherwise known as shirobasti, is an effective remedy for hair loss. Most Ayurvedic doctors and practitioners provide this form of therapy.

- The panchakarma treatment known as nasya, whereby medicated oil is poured into the nostrils, is also an ancient but highly effective remedy.

Brittle nails

According to Ayurveda, finger nails are a by-product of the bone tissue, so if your nails are brittle, split or ridged this may be a sign that your bone tissue is not being properly nourished.

Dietary guidelines

- We need calcium, zinc and magnesium for healthy bones and nails. A handful of sesame seeds every day delivers the recommended daily dose of calcium and magnesium, while pumpkin seeds and alfafa sprouts are excellent sources of zinc.
- If, after taking these foods, your nails are still brittle it is an indication that your digestion is being hampered by a build-up of ama in the GI tract, making it impossible for you to absorb these essential minerals. Triphala is an effective way to cleanse the GI tract of unwanted toxins and promote proper tissue nourishment (see Appendix 2 for suppliers). Take it before going to bed.

Cellulite

This is usually a Kapha problem and is also seen in people who use a lot of olive oil in their cooking.

Dietary guidelines

- Reduce the quantity of sweet, fatty foods in your diet as these hamper digestion and slow down the metabolic rate.
- Make sure you drink at least two lites of water every day.

Home remedies

- Massage the affected area daily with equal quantities of sesame oil and mustard oil. Alternatively you can use a dry body brush to stimulate the circulation.
- The Ayurvedic herb Gotu Kola (Centella asiatica) is a terrific natural remedy for cellulite. It works by boosting the circulation, but do be aware that you still need to adjust your diet and take more exercise for best results!

Lifestyle practices

- Increase your levels of exercise. This stimulates circulation and helps to break down the subcutaneous fat that accumulates, causing those telltale dimples on the thighs. Make sure the exercise you take actually works those areas of your body that are affected, such as your thighs and buttocks. Walking, swimming or jogging are good options, depending on your constitutional type and stage of life.

Chronic fatigue

Ayurveda treats this complex condition by restoring the digestive fire and rejuvenating the immunity (ojas).

Dietary guidelines

- To help build the digestive fire, chop up a piece of fresh ginger root, add a few drops of lime juice and a pinch of rock salt and chew this mixture before every meal.
- Make sure you drink plenty of hot water during the day and avoid iced and cold drinks at all times.
- Eat three good meals a day and avoid any type of fasting.
- Between meals, drink fresh vegetable and fruit juices to build your stamina and improve your tissue nourishment. A particularly energizing blend is made by juicing 4 carrots, 1 beetroot and an apple.
- After exercise, or any type of physical exertion, drink a cup of fresh orange juice with a pinch of rock salt.

Home remedies

- To build your stamina, take 2 figs, 3 dates, 3 almonds, 2 cardamom seeds and soak them overnight. Peel the almonds and cardamom seeds, deseed the dates then blend them together with 1 tsp of ghee and a glass of water. Drink this mixture every morning on an empty stomach.
- Alternatively, you might prefer to drink a rejuvenating cup of Ashwagandha tea every day (see Appendix 2 for suppliers). Simply steep 1 tsp of the powdered root in a cup of hot water for five to ten minutes before drinking.

Lifestyle practices

- Avoid strenuous forms of exercise, as this will further deplete your energy reserves and immunity. Instead, get into the habit of practising some gentle yoga asanas such as those given in Chapter 7.
- Practise Anulom lom daily, the method of alternate nostril breathing described in Chapter 8. It will fire up your digestion as well as helping to soothe, balance and nourish the mind with energy-giving oxygen.
- Practise meditation and methods of mind control.

Colds and flu

Most common in winter and spring, colds and flu are due to Kapha–Vata imbalances. The best natural remedy is fresh ginger root because it increases circulation, promotes sweating and digests any mucus, so relieving congestion. You can use it in a variety of ways but do not combine it with aspirin! Ginger and aspirin are both blood thinners so should never be taken together.

Dietary guidelines

- Eat sparingly and stick to foods that are simple, warm and easy to digest such as nourishing vegetable soups. Avoid all dairy products, fried foods, sweets, wheat and meat.
- Make sure you drink lots of hot water throughout the day to flush out your system and keep you well hydrated. Avoid cold and iced drinks of all kinds.
- In cases of chronic mucus, fasting on warm ginger water for two to three days gives a speedy recovery.

Home remedies

- Soak 2 parts fresh ginger root, 3 parts cinnamon and a pinch of cardamom in a cup of hot water for ten minutes and add $\frac{1}{2}$ tsp of honey before drinking this infusion. Take this tea several times a day.
- For colds with a cough, crush $\frac{1}{4}$ tsp fresh ginger root with 8 fresh basil leaves, 2 black peppercorns, 2 cardamom seeds, 1 cup of water, $\frac{1}{2}$ tsp turmeric powder, 2 cloves and 5 fresh mint leaves. Boil all the ingredients, filter and add 1 tsp of honey. Drink two to three times a day.
- Steep some fresh ginger root in a bowl of hot water, cover your head with a towel and use it as an inhalation to clear any nasal congestion.

Lifestyle practices

- Get plenty of rest and use the Bhastrika breath or Anulom lom breath described in Chapter 8 to help clear your sinuses and ease any lung congestion.
- Make sure you wrap up and keep warm.

Constipation

This is common in Vata types or whenever there is a Vata aggravation; it is due to an increase in hard, dry qualities in the body. If you suffer regularly from constipation it is very important for you to follow the daily routine prescribed in Chapter 7. In particular, make sure you drink a glass of hot water when you wake and regulate your bowel habits and meal times. In addition, the following practices give effective relief.

Dietary guidelines

- You need to follow a Vata-pacifying diet and make sure you avoid heavy foods such as wheat products and meat. Instead, increase your intake of high-fibre foods such as leafy green vegetables, oatmeal and fresh fruit. Bananas have a mildly laxative action; stewed apples, prunes, raisins and peaches are also useful.
- Drink at least two litres of water a day, served at room temperature or above.

Home remedies

- Triphala is the best Ayurvedic formula for constipation and is safe for long-term use. Do not take Triphala if you are pregnant.
- A simple home remedy is to dissolve 1 tsp of ghee in warm milk and drink it at night. This is safe for pregnant women but is not advisable if you have a Kapha constitution.
- Alternatively, try 1 tbsp of flaxseed in a cup of hot water at night. You will need to prepare the flaxseeds by either soaking them in a little water during the day or crushing them before use. Whichever method you choose, drink the whole cupful including the seeds!
- Castor oil is useful in stubborn cases, but should not be taken regularly as it is habit forming. Take 2 tsp at night in a cup of hot ginger tea or warm milk. If this fails to prompt a motion, increase the dose to a maximum of 4 tsp at night, but only for a few days.

Lifestyle practices

- Make sure you exercise for at least half an hour a day and practise your sun salutations as this stimulates the peristalsis movement.
- Practise pranayama, particularly the cleansing breath of Kapalabhati, as these methods of controlled breathing actually massage the intestines and so promote healthy elimination.

Coughs

There are many different kinds of cough, but in Ayurvedic terms they are all caused by a combination of aggravated Vata, Kapha and the accumulation of ama.

Dietary guidelines

Avoid sweets, wheat, icecream, cold drinks and dairy products as these all build Kapha and create ama.

Home remedies

- If the cough is dry, mix 1 tsp of turmeric powder with $\frac{1}{2}$ tsp of raw cane sugar and $\frac{1}{2}$ tsp of ghee. Take this concoction two to three times a day.
- Alternatively, take 1 tsp of licorice powder with 1 tsp of honey and a good pinch of freshly ground black pepper up to three times a day.
- For productive coughs, boil $\frac{1}{4}$ tsp fresh grated ginger root, 8 fresh basil leaves, 2 crushed black peppercorns, 2 crushed cardamom seeds, $\frac{1}{2}$ tsp of turmeric powder, 2 crushed cloves, 5 mint leaves and 1 cup of water. Simmer for a few minutes, filter, then add 1 tsp of honey and drink two to three times a day.
- Alternatively, you can mix 1 tsp of mustard powder and 1 tsp of dry ginger powder with 1 tsp of honey and take this concoction three times a day.

Cystitis

Ayurveda has several natural remedies to relieve this extremely painful condition.

Dietary guidelines

- Although you may not feel like it, be sure to drink plenty of fluid throughout the day. Cranberry juice is particularly beneficial.

Home remedies

- Make a tea from 1 tsp cumin powder, 1 tsp coriander powder, 1 tsp fennel seeds, $\frac{1}{4}$ tsp of dry ginger powder, 1 tsp raw cane sugar and 2 cups of water. Simmer together for two to three minutes, filter and drink half a cup two to three times a day.
- To relieve the burning sensation, make a paste from $\frac{1}{2}$ tsp ghee and $\frac{1}{8}$ tsp turmeric powder and apply it to the affected area repeatedly throughout the day, especially after urinating. Wear a sanitary towel to protect your clothing as the turmeric will stain!

Depression

This is a serious complaint. If you think you are suffering from depression consult your GP. The Ayurvedic remedies given here are safe to use in conjunction with any Western medical treatments, but do share this information with your doctor.

Depending on which dosha is aggravated, different types of depression occur. In a Vata depression, the cardinal symptoms are fear, anxiety, insomnia and intense feelings of loneliness or isolation. In Pitta, anger, self-criticism and fear of failure tend to be the dominant emotions. In Kapha types, weight gain, lethargy, excessive sleep and a general lack of interest in the world are the typical features. It is important to be able to recognize which type you are suffering from so you know which line of treatment to follow.

Whatever type of depression you are experiencing, it is vital you establish (and stick to) a wholesome daily routine, practise self-control and work on building your sense of self-esteem. Take care also to avoid becoming reliant on artificial stimulants such as alcohol and marijuana.

The Ayurvedic treatment of shirodhara described in Chapter 4 is also a very effective way to ease all types of depression and is available from most good Ayurvedic practitioners.

In Vata types of depression:

Dietary guidelines

- Follow a Vata-pacifying diet as described in Chapter 6.

Home remedies

- Make a tea from equal quantities of Ashwagandha and Brahmi (see Appendix 2 for suppliers) and drink this two to three times a day.
- Warm sesame oil and, using a nasal dropper or spoon, administer two to three drops into each nostril morning and evening on an empty stomach.
- At night add 1 tsp ghee and a pinch of nutmeg to a cup of warm milk and drink it just before bed.
- Massage 2 tbsp of sesame oil into your scalp at bedtime. Protect your pillow with a towel and wash the oil off in the morning.

Lifestyle practices

- You may not feel like being sociable, but do make the effort to get out and see your friends as much as you can. It will ease your feelings of isolation and help to put things in perspective.

- Be in touch with nature. Take a walk in the woods, go to the seaside, do some gardening. Nature restores us physically and mentally, causing our blood pressure to drop, heart rate to fall, muscles to relax, stress and anxiety to be greatly reduced.
- Take regular exercise; it releases endorphins or 'happy hormones' so will really lift your mood.
- Keep practising yoga in the mornings, especially the shoulder stand, cobra and spinal twists.
- Get into the habit of practising one of the methods of pranayama and meditation described in Chapter 8.

In Pitta types of depression:

Dietary guidelines

- Follow the Pitta-pacifying diet described in Chapter 6.

Home remedies

- Take 1 tsp of Gotu Kola powder with a cup of hot water twice daily.
- Put two to three drops of ghee into each nostril morning and evening on an empty stomach.
- Take 1 tsp of ghee and a pinch of nutmeg with warm milk at bedtime.
- Massage some cooling coconut or sunflower oil into the soles of your feet and your scalp at bedtime.

Lifestyle practices

- Use the cooling Shitali breath given in Chapter 8 and take time out to meditate for at least a few minutes every day. Meditating on a calm, tranquil visual image such as a beautiful lake can help to soothe feelings of anger and self-criticism.

In Kapha types of depression:

Dietary guidelines

- Follow the Kapha-pacifying diet described in Chapter 6.
- Drink fresh ginger root tea at least twice a day.
- A three- to four-day fast on apple juice is also great for lightening the load of a Kapha depression.

Lifestyle practices

- Do get up at a reasonable hour and take regular exercise. It will lift your mood and energize your whole system!

- Keep practising your yoga, especially the sun salutations, shoulder stand and plough.
- Get into the habit of using the Ujjayi breath of victory given in Chapter 8 to improve your mood.

Diabetes

Diabetes is a metabolic disorder caused by an imbalance of Kapha dosha. Ayurveda can help to manage this condition by improving the digestion, removing blockages which inhibit insulin uptake, lowering blood sugar levels, boosting metabolic functions and building overall immunity. In 80 per cent of cases, diabetes is acquired through an overindulgence in sweet, fatty foods and a sedentary lifestyle. It is essential, therefore, to start by eating the right foods and increasing your levels of activity.

Dietary guidelines

- First thing in the morning, drink a cup of hot water.
- Follow a Kapha-pacifying diet, making sure you avoid all sweet, fatty foods, especially sweets, refined carbohydrates, dairy products, refined sugars and other processed foods.
- Use plenty of digestive spices in your cooking, such as ginger, cumin, coriander and black pepper.
- Increase your intake of barley, spelt wheat and honey, which have a drying effect on the body.
- Drink a cup of hot water with fresh ginger root after every meal.

Home remedies

- To lower blood sugar levels, mix $\frac{1}{2}$ tsp of ground bay leaf with $\frac{1}{2}$ tsp of ground turmeric and 1 tbsp aloe vera juice. Take this mixture before lunch and dinner every day.
- Alternatively, 1 tsp of turmeric with 1 tsp of Amalaki (Emblica officinalis) and 1 tsp of honey is an effective home remedy.
- There are several Ayurvedic herbs that naturally reduce blood sugar levels. Guduci (Tinospora cordifolia) rejuvenates pancreas cells and works as a rasayana so helping to build overall strength and immunity; Meshashringi (Gymnema sylvestra) reduces blood sugar levels in both congenital and acquired (type 2) diabetes and also inhibits sweet tastes, so helps you to avoid the wrong types of foods!
- Rasayanas, such as Haritaki (Terminalia chebula), Amalaki and Triphala, are also good for building strength and normalizing metabolic functions.

- To get the right line of treatment for your particular needs, consult a qualified Ayurvedic doctor and keep your GP well informed of any remedies you decide to take.

Lifestyle practices

- Increase your levels of exercise. As well as helping to burn excess fat, exercise can improve insulin sensitivity.
- Certain yoga postures significantly improve blood sugar levels with sustained practice because they stimulate the pancreas to release more insulin. Useful asanas include the sun salutations, peacock pose, spinal twists and forward bends.

Diarrhoea

Diarrhoea is due to a Pitta imbalance, which weakens the digestive function. Common causes include overeating as well as eating stale or contaminated food. Ayurveda's approach is to restore the digestive fire and to destroy the progress of the condition by binding the bowel motions and preventing dehydration.

Useful foods

- Stew a couple of apples until they are very soft then add 1 tsp of ghee and a pinch of nutmeg. Eat this slowly, chewing each mouthful really well. It halts diarrhoea in its tracks and tastes great!
- Alternatively, mix a cup of cooked basmati rice with 1 tbsp of ghee and 3 tbsp of plain yoghurt and eat in small portions.

To prevent dehydration

- Juice a whole pomegranate, skin and all; add a little glucose and sip this mixture throughout the day. It stops diarrhoea and prevents dehydration.
- Drink small quantities of ginger tea throughout the day to keep your fluid levels up and restore your digestive fire.
- Add 1 tsp of raw natural sugar, 1 tsp of lime juice and a pinch of salt to a pint of warm water and drink this throughout the day.

Home remedies

- Mix $\frac{1}{4}$ tsp dry ginger powder, 1 tsp cumin powder, $\frac{1}{2}$ tsp raw natural sugar with $\frac{1}{2}$ cup of water. Drink this three to six times per day. If you suffer from acidity add 1 tsp of coriander powder to the mix.

Fever

The old saying, 'starve a fever', really does hold true! Ayurveda attributes fever to a chronic build-up of ama (undigested toxins) in the tissues of the body and a derangement of agni (digestive fire) which has left its normal seat in the stomach and migrated to the surface of the skin, hence the increased body temperature which is the cardinal symptom of fever. Once ama is removed and agni is returned to its seat, the fever will subside. The line of treatment, therefore, is to reduce toxicity by fasting and to use natural digestives to restore the digestive fire to its rightful place.

Dietary guidelines

- A total fast on warm ginger tea is recommended. Simply mix 1 tsp dry ginger powder in 5 glasses of water, bring to boil, filter and drink throughout the day.
- Alternatively, you can steep 1 tsp cumin seeds, 1 tsp coriander seeds and 1 tsp fennel seeds in a cup of hot water for ten minutes, strain and drink.
- Resist the temptation to drink iced or cold drinks as this will further reduce your already weak digestive fire.

Lifestyle practices

- Get plenty of rest and wrap yourself up warmly in a duvet or blanket to induce sweating as this will bring down the fever.
- Once the fever has subsided, follow a very simple diet to avoid upsetting your digestive system and eat small, regular meals to restore your strength. The post-fasting diet recommended in Chapter 4 is a good programme to follow at this time.

Flatulence

The colon is the seat of Vata and – being characterized by an excess of 'wind' – gas and flatulence are clearly Vata disorders!

Dietary guidelines

- Follow the Vata-pacifying diet described in Chapter 6.

Home remedies

- Immediately after eating, take 1 tsp of grated fresh ginger root mixed with 1 tsp of lime juice.
- Alternatively, mix 1 tsp of lemon juice with $\frac{1}{2}$ tsp of baking soda in a cup of water and drink this immediately after your meal.

Headaches

Headaches can be due to any one of the three doshas, so choose the remedy that suits your specific symptoms. In Vata types of headache the pain is usually of a throbbing nature and is confined to the back of the head, or starts at the back of the head and spreads to the front.

- Take a warm shower to relax and ease any muscular tension.
- Massage the shoulders with warm sesame oil.
- Make a paste from a little ground nutmeg and water, smooth it over your forehead and leave it on for about 30 minutes.

In Pitta-aggravated headaches, the pain is typically of a burning, penetrating kind and may be centralized or located around the temples. It is often associated with irritability and even nausea.

- Make a cooling paste from sandalwood powder and a little water and smear it over the forehead and temples.
- You can also boil $\frac{1}{2}$ tsp of ground cumin seeds and $\frac{1}{2}$ tsp of ground coriander seeds in a cup of hot water. Allow it to cool and then drink.

In Kapha types of headache there is usually nasal congestion due to colds or allergies.

- Make an inhalation using 10 drops of eucalyptus oil or fresh grated ginger root in a bowl of hot water, cover your head with a towel and inhale the steam.
- You can also ease the symptoms by applying a paste made from 1 tsp of dry ginger powder mixed with a little water to your forehead and sinus area. Alternatively, substitute the ginger with $\frac{1}{2}$ tsp of ground cinnamon powder.

Cooling yoga postures such as the moon salutations are useful for all types of headaches, but make sure you avoid any inverted postures as these increase the flow of blood to the head, so make the pain worse!

Hangover

Too much alcohol aggravates Pitta leading to headaches, nausea, dizziness and dehydration. These simple home remedies help to re-balance the system, giving rapid relief!

- Add 1 tsp of lime juice, $\frac{1}{2}$ tsp of raw cane sugar, $\frac{1}{2}$ tsp of baking soda and a pinch of rock salt to a glass of water. Stir and drink immediately.

- Alternatively, spice a glass of fresh orange juice with 1 tsp of lime juice and a pinch of cumin powder.

Heartburn and acid indigestion

This is usually due to overeating, combining incompatible foods (such as fish with milk or fruit with milk) or eating when you are upset. In each case the digestive fire is weakened, which causes food to sit and ferment in the stomach leading to indigestion and/or heartburn.

Dietary guidelines

- Follow a Pitta-pacifying diet, being careful to avoid hot, spicy and fermented foods as well as citrus fruits.
- Only eat when you are hungry and make sure you don't eat too much. At night allow at least three hours to elapse between your evening meal and going to bed.

Home remedies

- Add a pinch of baking soda to 2 tbsp of aloe vera juice for instant relief from heartburn and acidity.
- Alternatively, put $\frac{1}{2}$ tsp of baking soda in a cup, add ten drops of lime juice and $\frac{1}{2}$ teaspoon of organic sugar. The mixture will effervesce. Drink it immediately.

Lifestyle practices

- The cooling Shitali breath not only pacifies Pitta but also improves the digestion, so helping to relieve the underlying cause of heartburn and acidity.

Hypertension

This is a serious, potentially life-threatening condition so if you suspect you are suffering from raised blood pressure, consult your GP. The root cause of hypertension often lies in a person's diet and lifestyle. Too much salty food, stress, alcohol and smoking are all common triggers. Avoiding these factors and adopting some simple Ayurvedic practices, alongside any Western medical intervention, can help to get your blood pressure under control.

Avoid the causes

- Reduce your intake of salty foods.
- If you are a smoker and/or drink alcohol you need to cut down or, better still, stop altogether!

- Avoid working or exercising outdoors in the heat of the day.
- Adjust your lifestyle to minimize any physical and emotional stresses.

Dietary guidelines

- First thing in the morning drink honey water on an empty stomach. Simply add 1 tsp of honey and 5–10 drops of cider vinegar to a cup of hot water. This helps to reduce cholesterol and regulate blood pressure.
- Try drinking a cup of mango juice, followed an hour later by $\frac{1}{2}$ cup of warm milk flavoured with a pinch each of cardamom and nutmeg plus 1 tsp of ghee.
- Alternatively, mix 2 parts orange juice with 1 part coconut water and drink a cup of this mixture two to three times a day.

Home remedies

- Boil $\frac{1}{4}$ tsp of fenugreek seeds in a cup of hot water and drink this tea two to three times a day.
- Rub a little ghee on your temples and the soles of your feet during the day.

Lifestyle practices

- Meditation, pranayama and certain yogic postures can all help to lower blood pressure. Get into the habit of practising meditation daily, incorporating the Shitali breath, the corpse pose and moon salutations. Avoid inverted postures such as headstands and shoulder stands.

Ayurvedic therapies

- The soothing Ayurvedic therapy of shirodhara, where warm medicated oil is poured over the third eye (forehead), as described in Chapter 4, is a great way to ease tension and lower blood pressure. Most Ayurvedic practitioners offer this treatment.

Insomnia

Insomnia is due to an excess of Vata dosha. Ayurveda has some very simple remedies to promote a sound night's sleep.

Dietary guidelines

- Follow a Vata-pacifying diet and make sure you eat your evening meal as early as possible, at the very least two hours before going to bed.

Home remedies

- The Ayurvedic herb Ashwagandha (Withania somnifera) – which is widely available from suppliers of Ayurvedic remedies – is an age-old treatment for insomnia and a powerful nervine tonic.
- At bedtime, drink $\frac{1}{2}$ a cup of hot milk spiced with a pinch of ground nutmeg.

Lifestyle practices

- It is very important to establish a Vata-pacifying bedtime routine, starting with a warm (not hot) bath to ease any tension and help to prepare the mind for bed.
- Massage at least 2 tbsp of sesame oil into your scalp; protect your pillow with a towel and wash the oil off in the morning.
- Or make a paste using a few pinches of ghee and nutmeg and rub this gently into the forehead, temples and around the eyes for five to ten minutes before going to bed.
- Meditation is a terrific practice to master if you are prone to insomnia. Ten to fifteen minutes a day can soothe an overactive mind and resolve deep-rooted anxieties. It's particularly useful to practise meditation just before going to bed.

Irritable bowel syndrome (IBS)

Episodic cramping of the lower abdomen and fluctuating bouts of constipation and watery stools are the cardinal symptoms of IBS. It is a condition that affects twice as many women as men and is increasingly common in the Western world. Ayurveda attributes it to excessive levels of Vata and a build-up of ama (undigested toxins), which upset the body's natural ability to eliminate waste properly.

Dietary guidelines

- Avoid all heavy, stale and hard-to-digest foods such as oily, fried and raw foods, wheat, caffeine, refined white sugar, dairy foods and alcohol.
- Make sure you include plenty of digestive spices in your cooking such as cumin, coriander, ginger and black pepper.

Home remedies

- For seven days take 10mg of Haritaki (Terminalia chebula) before each meal. This mildly laxative herb is available from most good Ayurvedic suppliers. It will digest the sticky coating of ama which typically lines the GI tract in IBS, making bowel movements painful and erratic.

- Another simple remedy is to boil 1 tsp of flaxseed in a cup of water and drink it before going to bed.

Lifestyle practices

- Certain yoga postures can be used therapeutically to massage the intestines, increase blood flow to this area and promote normal bowel movements. Specific asanas to practise include the boat, spinal twists and forward bend.
- The complete abdominal breath described in Chapter 7 is a good exercise to practise daily as it gently massages the diaphragm and abdominal area, improving the blood flow and stimulating peristalsis.

Jetlag

Air travel increases the dry, light, mobile qualities in the body, leading to an aggravation of Vata dosha and the symptoms of jetlag. These simple remedies can help you to avoid it.

Dietary guidelines

- One of the causes of jetlag is dehydration. During the flight, make sure you drink two or more glasses of fresh water every couple of hours and avoid alcohol.
- On short trips there is really no need to eat the airline food, which is very hard to digest. On long-haul flights eat sparingly or, better still, take a thermos flask with you of home-made soup.

Home remedies

- The night before you fly – and for two days afterwards – take 1 tsp of castor oil in $\frac{1}{4}$ cup hot ginger tea at bedtime to cleanse your GI tract.

Lifestyle practices

- Take a warm bath and oil your body with sesame oil before and after the flight.

The menopause

The menopause is a natural part of the ageing process rather than an illness, but its symptoms can have a significant impact on a woman's quality of life. In Ayurvedic terms, it occurs as a woman moves from the Pitta to the Vata stage of life at around the age of 50. These simple practices can give tremendous relief.

Dietary guidelines

- Whatever your constitutional type, adopt the Vata-pacifying diet described in Chapter 6.

Home remedies

- The best Ayurvedic herb for the menopause is Shatavari (Asparagus racemosus). It is the natural alternative to HRT and has been used for thousands of years to safely and effectively relieve the common symptoms of the menopause such as hot flushes, irritability, mood swings, memory loss, dryness, weight gain and night sweats. Being rich in phytoestrogens, the plant world's equivalent of the female hormone oestrogen, it helps to re-balance the reproductive system.
- Organic rose-water spray is a wonderful way to soothe hot flushes.
- Hemp seeds can be added to your diet to relieve symptoms of dryness.
- Alternatively, take 1 tsp of fresh aloe vera juice three times a day.

Lifestyle practices

- Give yourself frequent oily massages with soothing sesame oil.
- Reduce all Vata-aggravating activities. This means less rushing around, keeping yourself warm and dry, avoiding any mental stress as much as you can and adopting a regular daily routine such as the one described in Chapter 7.

Menstrual problems

Menstrual problems can be due to a Vata, Pitta or Kapha imbalance. It is important to identify which dosha is out of balance for treatment to be effective. Whatever your constitutional type you can suffer from a Vata, Pitta or Kapha imbalance, so use your awareness to determine which dosha is responsible for your particular condition.

In Vata types of menstrual problems there will be pain and bloating in the lower abdomen and the menstrual flow is likely to be light or erratic. The best herb for this condition is Ashwagandha (Withania somnifera). Alternatively, try the following home remedy. Combine $\frac{1}{2}$ tsp of dill seed powder, $\frac{1}{4}$ tsp dry ginger powder, $\frac{1}{4}$ tsp ajwain powder, 1 pinch asafoetida, 1 tsp cumin seed powder, 1 tsp raw sugar cane and a glass of water. Boil these ingredients for five minutes; filter the decoction, allow it to cool and then add 1 tsp of aloe vera juice. Drink this decoction twice a day in the ten days prior to your menses and for the duration of your period.

In Pitta types the menstrual flow will be very heavy, hot flushes and irritability are likely and your breasts and bladder may be tender. Take Shatavari (Asparagus racemosus) to relieve these symptoms.

In Kapha types there is usually a heavy white discharge, more pain towards the end of the period, bloating, water retention and lethargy. Punanarva (Boerhavia diffusa) is the herb of choice for these symptoms.

Whatever your menstrual problem, taking 1 tbsp of aloe vera juice three times a day for the seven days before your period starts can prevent all types of menstrual pain and symptoms. You also need to follow the diet and yoga postures recommended for your particular constitutional type during this time. Sticking to these simple practices can mean you avoid period problems altogether!

Migraine

This is generally due to a Pitta imbalance, which causes the blood vessels around the brain to dilate, putting pressure on the nerves and causing pain and visual disturbances. Take action to reduce Pitta dosha.

Dietary guidelines

- Follow a Pitta-pacifying diet as described in Chapter 6. This can not only help to relieve migraines but is an effective method of prevention.
- If you tend to get migraines around midday (when Pitta dosha is at its peak) taking this simple home remedy at breakfast time can actually prevent it. Chop up a ripe banana, add 1 tsp of warm ghee, 1 tsp natural unrefined sugar, a pinch of cardamom and eat.

Home remedies

- At night take 1 tsp of castor oil before bed with a cup of warm water or ginger tea.
- During a migraine, make a Pitta-soothing tea with 1 tsp cumin powder and 1 tsp coriander powder.
- You can also help to relieve the symptoms by massaging cooling ghee into your temples.

Lifestyle practices

- All types of Pitta-pacifying activities are helpful in migraine, particularly the cooling Shitali breath given in Chapter 8 and the moon salutations illustrated in Chapter 7.

Obesity

The ancient Ayurvedic sages first wrote about obesity more than 5,000 years ago. It is a Kapha-related condition, so the first step in its management is to reduce your calorific intake and increase your levels of exercise. The following practices can help get obesity under control, but you also need to practise self-restraint and use your willpower!

Dietary guidelines

- Adopt the Kapha-pacifying diet described in Chapter 6 and increase your use of digestive herbs and spices such as ginger, black pepper, cumin and coriander to speed up your metabolism.
- Ideally skip breakfast altogether and eat just two meals a day. Alternatively, this natural energy drink makes a satisfying breakfast without piling on the pounds! Soak a handful of dates and almonds in water overnight with some fennel and cardamom seeds. Peel the almonds and blend all the ingredients together to make a low-fat, energizing smoothie.
- Drink fresh fruit and vegetable juices in between meals to satisfy any hunger pangs.
- If you must have a snack make sure it is a healthy one such as a handful of raisins, a carrot or stick of celery.
- Drink a glass of water with 1 tsp of honey daily.

Home remedies

- At night swallow $\frac{1}{2}$ tsp of whole fenugreek seeds with a cup of hot ginger tea. This helps to reduce triglycerol and LDL cholesterol levels in the body.
- Or you might prefer to take the following herbal remedy three times a day for one month. Combine 1 tsp cumin seeds, 1 tsp of dry ginger powder, $\frac{1}{4}$ tsp ajwain, $\frac{1}{4}$ tsp rock salt and a pinch of asafoetida in a glass of warm water.
- The Ayurvedic remedy Guggulu (Commiphora mukul), taken with 1 tsp of honey, has been used for thousands of years to treat obesity. Triphala, the Ayurvedic compound formulation, also promotes weight loss (see Appendix 2 for suppliers).

Lifestyle practices

- Avoid napping during the day; it slows down your metabolism!
- Include the Bhastrika breath described in Chapter 8 in your daily routine. It increases the metabolic rate, so burns calories.
- Make sure you take regular, high-impact exercise such as jogging and aerobics. If you can't manage this then at least build half an hour of fast walking or swimming into your daily routine.

Osteoporosis

This is most common in older women because, after the menopause, little or no oestrogen is produced. Oestrogen is needed to convert calcium, magnesium, zinc and other essential building blocks into bone tissue. From an Ayurvedic point of view, osteoporosis is explained by the fact that, once we hit 55 years of age, Vata dosha takes control. Being made up of air and ether this increases the porous quality of our bones. The good news is that osteoporosis can be managed, and even prevented, by dietary measures and some gentle exercise.

Dietary guidelines

- Follow the Vata-pacifying diet outlined in Chapter 6 and ideally avoid eating any meat products. Numerous clinical studies have found that a vegetarian diet is one of the best ways to prevent osteoporosis.
- Chew a handful of sesame seeds every day. Sesame seeds are rich in calcium, so help to prevent osteoporosis without clogging your arteries!
- Other natural sources of calcium include all types of seaweed, quinoa, parsley, hazelnuts, cow's, goat's and soya milk products, so make sure you include these in your regular diet.
- You can also take a glass of almond milk before breakfast and at bedtime. Simply soak a handful of almonds overnight, peel them and blend with a glass of cow's, goat's or soya milk and add a pinch each of cardamom, ginger powder and saffron.

Home remedies

- The rejuvenating herb Shatavari (Asparagus racemosus) is useful in osteoporosis because it contains natural precursors to the female hormone oestrogen, which helps to improve the body's ability to metabolize calcium and build healthier bones.

Lifestyle practices

- Diet alone is not sufficient to prevent osteoporosis. A little gentle exercise is essential to help stimulate the metabolism to produce bone tissue. Take care, however, to avoid activities such as weight lifting, which put stress on already fragile bones. Instead, go for a gentle 30-minute stroll or try swimming.

- If you are already suffering from osteoporosis yoga postures should be performed with great care. If in doubt seek the advice of a yoga teacher or stick to walking or swimming.

Skin problems

Ayurveda has many remedies to help heal skin problems or simply to promote a beautiful, natural complexion.

For dry skin

- Make sure you drink plenty of water, at least two litres a day at room temperature or above.

- Massage your skin regularly with the oil best suited to your constitutional type (sesame oil for Vata types, sunflower oil for Pitta types, corn oil for Kapha types).

- Make a nourishing face pack by blending a handful of fresh cherries to a pulp and applying this to your face for 15 minutes before bedtime.

For psoriasis

- Mix 100 g ghee, 10 g of turmeric powder, 5 g of licorice powder, 30 ml of sesame oil and 5 ml of neem oil (available from many health food shops and suppliers of Ayurvedic remedies). Warm the ingredients and then massage into the affected area. Leave it on for a few minutes before washing off. Apply this three times a week for best results.

For rashes and hives

- For immediate relief from rashes due to allergies or insect bites, blend a handful of fresh coriander leaves to a pulp and smooth the paste over the affected area. You can drink the remaining juice.

- Applying cooling melon juice or aloe vera juice over the affected area can also give rapid relief.

For urticaria

- Make a paste from 1 pinch of black pepper and $\frac{1}{2}$ tsp of ghee and eat this concoction in the morning on an empty stomach. You will need to take this daily for several months to resolve this deep-rooted skin problem.

For wrinkles and pimples

- Make a face pack from 1 banana, $\frac{1}{4}$ tsp ghee, 1 tsp sesame seeds, 2 almonds and enough water to make a paste. Put everything in a blender and apply to the affected area. Leave it on for at least 30 minutes then wash off. Apply daily before bed.

For a healthy, natural complexion

- In Sanskrit the word for turmeric means: 'that which beautifies the skin'. It's a spice that has been used for centuries to improve skin quality, so get in the habit of taking a capsule of turmeric every day (see Appendix 2 for suppliers) for a lustrous, healthy complexion.

- Take ten minutes morning and night to cleanse, massage and moisturize your skin. Ghee is a natural cleanser and moisturiser and great for removing all vestiges of make-up. If you don't like the smell then substitute it for the oil best suited to your constitutional type (sesame oil for Vata, sunflower oil for Pitta, corn oil for Kapha types).

- Give yourself a daily all-over massage with the oil best suited to your constitutional type to preserve the texture of your skin, improve circulation and prevent cellulite.

- If your skin is very pale it may be a sign that you are not getting enough iron, so drink a glass of carrot juice every day and notice how it improves your skin tone.

- Be sparing with your use of soap as it strips the skin of its natural oils. As a general rule, you really only need to wash with soap twice a week. Pitta types may need to use soap a little more frequently as their skin tends to be more oily.

- Wash in cool water if you are Pitta, warm water if you have a Vata or Kapha constitution.

Sore throat

This complaint is easily treated using Ayurvedic home remedies.

- Gargle morning and evening with $\frac{1}{2}$ tsp turmeric and $\frac{1}{2}$ tsp of salt dissolved in a cup of warm water.

- Make a soothing herbal tea with $\frac{1}{2}$ tsp of grated fresh ginger root, $\frac{1}{2}$ tsp of ground cinnamon stick, $\frac{1}{2}$ tsp of crushed licorice root. Drink it up to three times a day.

Stomach ache

Dietary guidelines

- Follow a light diet of home-made vegetable soups or plain boiled rice and drink plenty of fresh ginger root tea after each meal.

Home remedies

- Combine $\frac{1}{3}$ tsp of ground cumin powder, a pinch of asafoetida and a pinch of rock salt. Chew it well and wash down with warm water.
- Or, dry roast $\frac{1}{2}$ tsp fennel seeds, $\frac{1}{2}$ tsp of cumin seeds and $\frac{1}{2}$ tsp of coriander seeds. Mix them together and chew about $\frac{1}{2}$ tsp of this mixture at intervals throughout the day.
- Another remedy is to mix $\frac{1}{2}$ tsp of ajwain powder with $\frac{1}{2}$ tsp of baking soda. Chew this mixture and wash it down with a cup of warm water.

Stress

We all experience stress in our daily lives. Here are some tools you can use to reduce its impact on your mental and physical wellbeing.

Home remedies

- Give yourself a massage with sesame seed oil if you are a Vata type, sunflower oil if you are Pitta predominant and corn oil if you are a Kapha type of person.
- Take a relaxing hot bath with $\frac{1}{3}$ cup fresh ginger and $\frac{1}{3}$ cup baking soda. Soak yourself in it for 10–15 minutes.
- Make a stress-busting tea with soothing chamomile or $\frac{1}{2}$ tsp of Brahmi powder (Herpestis monnieri), which is available from most good suppliers of Ayurvedic remedies (see Appendix 2).

Lifestyle practices

- Good yoga postures to practise include the shoulder stand, plough, spinal twists and the lion pose.
- Practise meditation and the Ujjayi breath described in Chapter 8 to help melt away feelings of tension and anxiety.

- Accept the stresses you can't change and do something about the ones you can!
- Don't let yourself to get bogged down in negative patterns of thought. Instead, try replacing them with more positive thoughts. Refer back to Chapter 3 for more details on how to achieve this.
- Let out your emotions – having a good laugh or cry are great stress busters!
- Take a little time out of your day to relax, unwind and be with nature if you can, it really does help to soothe over-anxious minds.

The next step

Congratulations on making the effort to read *Teach yourself Ayurveda*. You are now equipped with the knowledge you need to create a healthy, Ayurvedic way of life.

As you will have realized, Ayurveda is not a quick fix or a magic bullet: for its benefits to be felt you need to make some sincere and perhaps challenging adjustments to many aspects of your lifestyle. It is hoped that the insights you have gained from this book will inspire you to start making those changes.

The easiest way to get started is to get to grips with your mind–body type and make some adjustments to your diet. Remember to keep a record of these changes, and how they make you feel, in your diary so you can monitor the progress you are making. As you start to see and feel the benefits, it is hoped that this will prompt you to make more changes to your lifestyle, such as getting up a little earlier, taking steps to combat the impact of each new season and building healing yoga practices, pranayama and meditation into your daily routine.

In the final section of this book you will find useful resources and further information you can use to expand your knowledge, understanding and practice of Ayurveda still further, should you wish.

Namaste (I bow to the god within you)!

part

three

taking it further

Vata

Dairy foods to eat

Most organic dairy foods and dairy substitutes are good for Vata, including:

Butter	Hard cheeses (in moderation)
Buttermilk	Soft cheeses
Cow's milk	Natural yoghurt
Rice milk	(diluted and spiced)
Goat's milk	Ice cream (occasionally)
Ghee (clarified butter)	Sour cream

Dairy foods and dairy substitutes to avoid

Powdered milk products
Soya milk
Yoghurt (frozen and with fruit varieties)

Animal products to eat

Chicken (dark meat is best)	Turkey (dark meat is best)
Duck	Seafood
Eggs	Venison
Fresh fish	

Animal products to avoid

Beef	Lamb
Pork	Rabbit
Veal	

Grains to eat

Amaranth
Buckwheat (must be well
  cooked and flavoured
  with ghee)
Millet (must be well cooked
  and flavoured with ghee)
Oats (cooked)
Quinoa
Wholegrain wheat (ideally
  spelt or kamut varieties)
Wheat-free pasta
Rice (all varieties,
  particularly basmati)
Rye (must be well cooked
  and flavoured with ghee)

Grains to avoid

Barley
Bread (with yeast)
Corn
Couscous
Oat bran
Oats (raw)
Polenta
Pasta made with wheat
Rice cakes (unless they
  are eaten with oily substances
  such as butter, ghee, honey
  or jam)

Pulses to eat

Stick to the lighter varieties of pulses.
Black lentils
Red lentils
Mung beans
Mung dal
Tofu (marinated)
Tur dal
Urad dal

Pulses to avoid

Aduki beans
Black beans
Black-eyed peas
Brown lentils
Chickpeas
Kidney beans
Butter/Lima beans
Miso
Peas (dried)
Soya beans
Split peas
Tempeh
White beans

Vegetables to eat

Generally, cooked vegetables are best.

Asparagus
Beetroot
Carrots (cooked)
Celery (cooked)
Courgettes (zucchini)
Cucumber
Fennel
Garlic
Green beans
Leafy greens

Leeks
Okra
Olives
Onions (cooked)
Mustard greens
Parsnips
Peas (cooked)
Pumpkin
Radishes (cooked)
Spinach (if eaten raw, take at lunchtime with oily dressing)

Salad leaves (only at lunchtime with oily dressing)
Squash and marrow (cooked with ghee and mildly spiced)
Swede
Sweet potato
Watercress

Vegetables to avoid

Generally, avoid frozen and raw vegetables.

Artichokes
Aubergine (eggplant)
Broccoli
Brussels sprouts
Burdock root
Bell peppers
Cabbage
Carrots (raw)
Cauliflower
Celery (raw)

Corn/sweet corn
Dandelion greens
Kale
Kohlrabi
Mushrooms
Radishes (raw)
Tomatoes
Turnips
White potatoes

Fruits to eat

Apples (only if cooked with warming spices)
Apricots
Avocado
Berries (most sweet varieties)
Bananas (ripe)
Cantaloupe melon
Cherries
Dates
Figs (fresh not dried)
Grapes (all varieties)
Grapefruit
Kiwi
Lemon

Lime
Mango (when ripe, in moderation)
Melons
Oranges
Papaya
Peaches
Pears (cooked)
Pineapple
Plums
Prunes (soaked not dried)
Raisins (soaked)
Rhubarb
Tamarind

Fruits to avoid

Generally avoid all dried and unripe fruits.

Apples (raw)	Pomegranate
Cranberries	Raisins (unsoaked)
Dates (dried)	Raspberries
Pears	Strawberries
Persimmon	Watermelon

Nuts and seeds to eat

Generally all are good in moderation, but they should be ground or soaked before eating.

Almonds (soaked and peeled)	Walnut
Brazil	Flax seeds
Cashew	Psyllium seeds
Coconut	Pumpkin seeds
Hazelnut	Safflower seeds
Macadamia	Sesame seeds
Pecan	Sunflower seeds
Pine nut	Tahini
Pistachio	

Nuts and seeds to avoid

Generally avoid all forms of salted nuts, particularly:
Peanuts
Popcorn

Oils to eat

Most are suitable, particularly:

Ghee
Olive oil
Sesame oil

Oils to avoid

Canola oil
Corn oil

Sweeteners

All are good except white sugar.

Herbs and spices to eat

Virtually all are good, particularly:

Ajwain	Cloves
Allspice	Cumin
Anise	Dill
Asafoetida (hingu)	Fennel
Basil	Fenugreek (in moderation)
Bay leaves	Garlic
Black pepper	Ginger
Cardamom	Nutmeg
Coriander (cilantro)	Turmeric
Cinnamon	

Condiments to eat

Chocolate (in moderation)	Pickles
Kelp	Salt (in moderation)
Lime pickle	Soya sauce
Mango chutney	Tamari
Mayonnaise	Vinegar (in moderation)
Mustards	

Condiments to avoid

Horseradish
Chilli pepper (too drying!)
Ketchup

Drinks to enjoy

Almond milk	Wine (in moderation,
Aloe vera juice	with or after a meal)
Apple cider	Chamomile tea
Apricot juice	Clove tea
Berry juice (except cranberry)	Elderflower tea
Carob	Eucalyptus tea
Carrot juice	Fennel tea
Grain coffee substitutes	Ginger tea (made with
Grapefruit juice	fresh ginger root)
Grape juice	Juniper berry tea
Lemonade	Lavender tea
Mango juice	Lemongrass tea
Orange juice	Licorice tea
Papaya juice	Peppermit tea
Pineapple juice	Rosehip tea
Rice milk	Sarsaparilla tea
Vegetable bouillon	Spearmint tea

Drinks to avoid

Generally avoid all cold and iced drinks.

Apple juice
Beer
Black tea
Coffee and caffeinated drinks
Carbonated drinks
Chocolate-flavoured milk
Cranberry juice
Pear juice
Pomegranate juice
Prune juice
Soya milk

Tomato juice
Vegetable juices (like V-8)
Blackberry tea
Borage tea
Dandelion tea
Ginseng tea
Hibiscus tea
Nettle tea
Passionflower tea
Red Zinger
Yarrow tea

Pitta

Dairy foods to eat

Butter (unsalted)
Cheese (soft not hard)
Cottage cheese
Cow's milk

Ghee
Goat's milk
Ice cream
Yoghurt (if fresh and diluted)

Dairy foods to avoid

Butter (salted)
Buttermilk
Cheese (hard, aged)
Yoghurt (plain, fruit, frozen)

Animal products to eat

Chicken (white meat)
Eggs (whites only)
Fish (freshwater)
Rabbit

Shrimp (in moderation)
 is best)
Turkey (white meat)
Venison

Animal products to avoid

Beef
Chicken (dark meat)
Duck
Egg (yolks)
Fish (seawater)

Lamb
Pork
Seafood
Turkey (dark meat)

Grains to eat

Amaranth
Barley
Oat bran
Oats (cooked)
Quinoa
Rice (all varieties except brown rice)
Wheat-based pasta (if not intolerant to wheat)
Rice cakes
Wheat (wholegrain, spelt and kamut varieties are best)

Grains to avoid

Bread (with yeast)
Brown rice
Buckwheat
Corn
Millet
Rye

Pulses to eat

Generally good in moderation.

Aduki beans
Black beans
Black-eyed peas
Chickpeas (well cooked or as humous)
Mung beans
Mung dal
Peas (dried)
Pinto beans
Red and yellow lentils
Soya beans
Tempeh
Tofu
White beans

Pulses to avoid

Butter/Lima beans
Kidney beans
Miso
Soya sauce
Tur dal
Urad dal

Vegetables to eat

Generally choose sweet, bitter and astringent-tasting vegetables.

Asparagus
Artichoke
Beetroot (cooked)
Broccoli
Brussels sprouts
Cabbage
Carrots (cooked)
Cauliflower
Celery
Coriander leaf
Courgette (zucchini)
Cucumber
Dandelion greens
Fennel
Garlic (cooked)
Green beans
Kale
Leeks (cooked)
Lettuce
Mushrooms

Okra
Onions (cooked never raw)
Parsnip
Peas
Pumpkin
Radishes

Squash and marrow
Swede
Sweet potatoes
Watercress
White potatoes

Vegetables to avoid

Generally avoid sour, pungent-tasting vegetables.

Beetroot (raw)
Burdock root
Corn/sweetcorn
Eggplant (aubergine)
Garlic (raw)
Green chillies
Horseradish
Kohlrabi
Leeks (raw)

Mustard greens
Olives
Onions (raw)
Peppers
Radishes (raw)
Spinach (cooked)
Spring onions
Tomatoes
Turnips

Fruit to eat

Generally choose sweet-tasting fruits.

Apples (ripe)
Apricots
Avocados
Bananas
Berries (sweet varieties)
Cherries
Cocnuts
Dates
Figs
Grapes (red and black varieties)
Lime (occasionally)
Mangoes (ripe)

Melons
Oranges (occasionally)
Papayas
Pears
Pineapples (when very ripe/sweet)
Plums (when very ripe)
Pomegranates
Prunes (soaked)
Raisins
Raspberries (occasionally)
Strawberries (occasionally, when very sweet)

Fruit to avoid

Generally choose sour and unripe fruit.

Apples (unripe)
Berries (when sour)
Cranberries
Grapefruit
Grapes (green)

Kiwi
Lemons
Mangoes (green)
Oranges (when sour)
Peaches

Persimmon   Rhubarb
Pineapples   Tamarind
Plums

Nuts and seeds to eat

Almonds (only when   Pumpkin seeds
  soaked and peeled)   (occasionally)
Coconut   Safflower seeds
Popcorn (no salt, but can   (occasionally)
  add unsalted butter)   Sunflower seeds
Psyllium seeds   (occasionally)

Nuts and seeds to avoid

All other types of nuts and seeds are too hot and oily for
Pitta types.

Oils to eat

Canola oil   Olive oil
Coconut oil   Soya oil
Ghee   Sunflower oil

Oils to avoid

Almond oil   Sesame oil
Corn oil   Walnut oil
Safflower oil

Sweeteners

All are good in moderation except white sugar, honey and
molasses.

Herbs and spices to eat

Generally choose more cooling varieties.

Aniseed   Fennel
Basil leaves (fresh)   Ginger (fresh)
Black pepper   Mint
  (in small amounts)   Parsley (in moderation)
Caraway (in small amounts)   Peppermint
Cardamom (in small amounts) Saffron
Cinnamon   Spearmint
Coriander (cilantro)   Tarragon (in small amounts)
Cumin   Turmeric
Dill

Herbs and spices to avoid

Ajwain
Allspice
Anise
Asafoetida (hingu)
Basil (dried)
Bay leaves
Cayenne pepper
Cloves
Fenugreek

Ginger (dried)
Mace
Marjoram
Mustard seeds
Nutmeg
Oregano
Paprika
Rosemary

Condiments to eat

Chocolate (in moderation)
Sweet mango chutney
Tamari (in small amounts)

Condiments to avoid

Chilli pepper
Horseradish
Kelp
Ketchup
Lime pickle
Hot mango chutney
Mango pickle

Mayonnaise
Mustard
Pickles
Salt (in excess)
Seaweed
Soya sauce
Vingear

Drinks to enjoy

Beer (occasionally)
Almond milk
Aloe vera juice
Apple juice
Apricot juice
Berry juice (if sweet)
Carob
Cool dairy drinks
Grain coffee substitutes
Grape juice
Mango juice
Mixed vegetable juice
Peach juice
Orange juice (in small
quantities)
Pomegranate juice
Prune juice
Rice milk
Soya milk

Vegetable bouillon
Black tea
Blackberry tea
Borage tea
Burdock tea
Chamomile tea
Chicory tea
Dandelion tea
Fennel tea
Ginger tea
Hibiscus tea
Jasmine tea
Lemongrass tea
Licorice tea
Nettle tea
Passionflower tea
Peppermint tea
Sarsparilla tea
Spearmint tea

Drinks to avoid

Alcohol (spirits)
Cider
Wine
Berry juice (sour)
Carbonated drinks
Carrot juice
Chocolate milk drinks
Coffee and caffeinated
  drinks
Cranberry juice

Grapefruit juice
Ice-cold drinks
Iced tea and coffee
Tomato juice
Clove tea
Fenugreek tea
Ginseng tea
Rosehip tea
Red Zinger

Kapha

Dairy foods to eat

Generally, dairy foods should be eaten sparingly.

Buttermilk (in moderation)
Cottage cheese (only made
  from skimmed goat's milk)
Ghee (in moderation;
  alternatively flaxseed oil)

Goat's cheese
  (fresh, unsalted)
Goat's milk (skimmed)

Dairy foods to avoid

Butter (salted – unsalted
  can be eaten very
  occasionally)
Cheese (soft and hard)

Cow's milk
Ice cream
Sour cream
Yoghurt (all varieties)

Animal products to eat

Chicken (white meat)
Eggs
Fish (freshwater,
  in moderation)

Rabbit
Seafood (in moderation)
Turkey (white meat)
Venison

Animal products to avoid

Beef
Chicken (dark meat)
Duck
Fish (seawater varieties)

Lamb
Pork
Turkey (dark meat)

Grains to eat

Generally grains should be eaten sparingly.

Amaranth (occasionally)
Barley
Brown basmati rice
Buckwheat
Corn
Millet
Oat bran

Oats (dried)
Polenta
Quinoa (in moderation)
Rye
Spelt wheat (occasionally)
Wild rice

Grains to avoid

Bread (with yeast)
Oats (cooked)
Pasta (wheat-based)
White rice

Wheat (particularly
products made with
durum wheat flour)

Pulses to eat

Aduki beans
Black beans
Black eyed peas
Chickpeas
Lentils (brown and red)
Butter/Lima beans
Mung beans (in moderation)
Mung dal (in moderation)

Peas (dried)
Pinto beans
Soya milk
Split peas
Tempeh
Tofu (cooked, occasionally)
Tur dal
White beans

Pulses to avoid

Black lentils
Kidney beans
Miso
Soya beans

Soya sauce
Tofu (cold)
Urad dal

Vegetables to eat

Generally eat cooked vegetables rather than raw.

Artichokes
Asparagus
Beetroot
Broccoli
Brussels sprouts
Burdock root
Cabbage

Carrots
Cauliflower
Celery
Corn/sweetcorn
Courgette (zucchini)
Dandelion leaves
Fennel

Garlic
Green beans
Green chillies
Horseradish
Kale
Kolhrabi
Leafy greens
Leeks
Lettuce
Marrow
Mushrooms
Mustard greens

Okra
Onions
Parsley
Peas
Peppers (hot and sweet)
Potatoes
Pumpkin
Radishes
Swede
Spinach
Squash
Tomatoes (cooked not raw)

Vegetables to avoid

Mainly juicy, cold and sweet varieties as well as root vegetables.

Aubergine (eggplant)
Cucumber
Olives
Parsnips (can have occasionally)

Sweet potatoes
Tomatoes (raw)
White potatoes

Fruit to eat

Go for the lighter, more astringent-tasting fruits.

Apples
Apricots
Berries
Cherries
Cranberries
Figs (dried, in moderation)
Grapes (in moderation)
Lemons and limes
  (in moderation)

Mangoes (occasionally)
Peaches
Pears
Pomegranates
Prunes
Raisins
Strawberries (in moderation)

Fruits to avoid

Mainly avoid very heavy, juicy fruits.

Avocados
Bananas
Coconuts
Dates
Figs (fresh)
Grapefruit
Kiwi

Melons
Oranges
Papayas
Pineapple
Plums
Rhubarb
Watermelon

Nuts and seeds

Basically avoid them all; they are too oily and heavy.

Oils to eat

Use as little as possible of any variety.

Almond oil	Flaxseed oil
Canola oil	Ghee (in moderation)
Corn oil	Sunflower oil

Oils to avoid

Coconut oil	Sesame oil
Olive oil	Soya oil
Safflower oil	Walnut oil

Sweeteners

Avoid all sweeteners except honey.

Herbs and spices

All herbs and spices are good for Kapha.

Condiments to eat

Chilli pepper
Horseradish
Hot mango chutney
Mustard

Condiments to avoid

Chocolate	Pickles
Kelp	Salt
Ketchup	Soya sauce
Lime pickle	Tamari
Sweet mango chutney	Vinegar
Mayonnaise	

Drinks to enjoy

Cider	Aloe vera juice
Red and white wine	Apricot juice*
Spirits (diluted,	Black tea (spiced)
in moderation)	Carob

Carrot juice
Coffee and caffeinated
  drinks (very occasionally)
Cranberry juice*
Grain coffee substitutes
Grape juice*

Peach juice*
Pear juice
Prune juice*
Soya milk (hot and
  well spiced)

*Fruit juices should be diluted half-and-half with water.

Chamomile tea
Chicory tea
Cinnamon tea
Clove tea
Dandelion tea
Fenugreek tea
Ginger tea
Hibiscus tea

Jasmine tea
Lavender tea
Lemongrass tea
Nettle tea
Peppermint tea
Spearmint tea
Yarrow tea

Drinks to avoid

Beer
Sweet wine
Almond milk
Carbonated drinks
Chocolate milk drinks
Cold dairy drinks
Grapefruit juice
Ice-cold drinks
Iced tea and coffee

Lemonade
Miso broth
Orange juice
Papaya juice
Rice milk
Soya milk (cold)
Tomato juice
Red Zinger tea

Useful contacts in Australia

Industry associations

Australasian Association of Ayurveda Incorporated
Tel: +61 (0)8 8366 6516
Email: austerba@senet.com.au

Australian Natural Therapists Association
ANTA National Administration Office
PO Box 657
Maroochydore
Queensland 4558
Freecall: 1800 817 577
Tel: +61 (0)7 5409 8222
Fax: +61 (0)7 5409 8200
Email: **anta1955@bigpond.com**
Website: **www.anta.com.au**

Suppliers of Ayurvedic remedies

Ayurveda Elements
17 Orchard Rd
Chatswood
NSW 2067
Tel: +61 (0)2 9904 7754
Email: **ayurveda@iinet.net.au**
Website: **www.ayurvedaelements.com**

Mullumbimby Herbals
79 Stuart St
Mullumbimby
NSW 2482
Tel: +61 (0)2 6684 3002
Email: orders@mullumherbals.com
Website: www.mullumherbals.com

Nu-Looks Imports
PO Box 3203
Caroline Springs
Victoria 3023
Tel: +61 (0)3 8361 8138
Fax: +61 (0)3 8361 8102
Email: nulooks@bigpond.net.au
Website: www.ayurhealth.com.au

Useful contacts in New Zealand

Industry association

New Zealand Ayurvedic Association Inc
PO Box 36171
Northcote
North Shore City 0748
Website: www.ayurveda.org.nz

Suppliers of Ayurvedic remedies

Lambs Pharmacy
173 Karangahape Rd
Newton
Auckland
Tel: +64 (0)79-377 4230
Fax: +64 (0)79-377 4232
Email: lambs@naturaltherapies.co.nz

Wellpack College of Natural Therapies
Ayurvedic Dispensary
6 Francis Street
Grey Lynn
Auckland
Tel: +64 (0)79-360 0560
Fax: +64 (0)79-376 4307
Email: dispensary1@wellpark.co.nz
Website: www.wellpark.co.nz

Useful contacts in the UK

Industry association

The Ayurvedic Practitioners Association
34 Featherstone Road
Mill Hill
London
NW7 2BN
Tel: +44 (0)7983 124950
Email: info@apa.uk.com
Website: www.apa.uk.com

Suppliers of Ayurvedic remedies

Essential Ayurveda
The Old Plough
Fen Road
Halton Holegate
Lincs
PE23 5PF
Tel: +44(0)1754 830559
Email: andy@essentialayurveda.co.uk
Website: www.essentialayurveda.co.uk

Indigo Herbal Ltd
PO Box No. 22317
London
W13 8WE
Tel: +44(0)208 621 3633
Email: info@indigoherbal.co.uk
Website: www.indigoherbal.co.uk

Maharishi Ayurveda Products (MAP)
Beacon House
Willow Walk
Skelmersdale
Lancashire
WN8 6UR
Tel: +44(0)1695 51015
Fax: +44 (0)1695 50917
Email: map@maharishi.co.uk
Website: www.maharishi.co.uk

Pukka Herbs
The Old Sawmill
Home Farm
Barrow Court Lane
Barrow Gurney
Bristol
BS48 3RW
Tel: +44(0)1275 461950
Email: **info@pukkaherbs.com**
Website: **www.pukkaherbs.com**

Vedic Medical Hall Ltd
6 Chiltern Street
London
W1U 7PT
Tel: +44(0)207 935 0028
Fax: +44(0)207 935 6971
Email: **info@vedicmedicalhall.com**
Website: **www.vedicmedicalhall.com**

Other useful contacts

BWY Central Office
The British Wheel of Yoga
25 Jermyn Street
Sleaford
Lincolnshire
NG34 7RU
Tel: +44(0)1529 306851
Fax: +44(0)1529 303233
Email: **office@bwy.org.uk**
Website: **www.bwy.org.uk**

Maharishi Ayurveda Health Centres
Tel: +44(0)1695 51008
Fax: +44(0)1695 720325
Email: **mahc@maharishi.co.uk**
Website: **www.maharishiayurveda.co.uk**

Useful contacts in USA

Industry association and supplier contact

The following industry association provides both a registry of Ayurvedic practitioners and a list of authentic suppliers of Ayurvedic herbal remedies via its website.

National Ayurvedic Medical Association
620 Cabrillo Avenue
Santa Cruz
CA 95065
Email: **info@ayurveda-nama.org**
Website: **www.ayurveda-nama.org**

The Ayurvedic Cookbook, Amadea Morningstar, Lotus Press, Wisconsin, 1990

Ayurvedic Cooking for Self-Healing, Dr Vasant Lad and Usha Lad, The Ayurvedic Press, Albuquerque, 1997

Ayurveda and the Mind, Dr David Frawley, Lotus Press, Wisconsin, 1996

Ayurvedic Healing, Dr David Frawley, Morson Publishing, Salt Lake City, 1989

Ayurveda: Life, Health and Longevity, Dr Robert E. Svoboda, Penguin, London, 1992

Ayurveda Secrets of Healing, Maya Tiwari, Lotus Press, Wisconsin, 1998

Healing with Whole Foods, Paul Pitchford, North Atlantic Books, 2002

Heaven's Banquet, Miriam Kasin Hospodar, Penguin Group, 1999

Prakruti, Your Ayurvedic Constitution, Dr Robert E. Svoboda, Geocom Ltd, Albuquerque, 1989

The Science of Self-Healing, Dr Vasant Lad, Lotus Press, Santa Fc, 1984

Therapeutic Yoga, Dr Ali and Jiwan Brar, Random House, 2002

The Yoga of Herbs, Dr David Frawley and Dr Vasant Lad, Lotus Press, Santa Fe, 1986

Abhyanga   A form of oily massage in which therapeutic oils are applied to the body in synchronized strokes.

Agni   The factor responsible for the processes of digestion and metabolism.

Ama   Undigested food toxins that accumulate in the GI tract due to inadequate digestion and which are the root cause of many diseases. The term is also used to describe mental and emotional toxins that accumulate in the system and create a barrier to normal bodily and mental functions.

Amapachana   The term used to decribe any herbal medicines used to digest ama in the GI tract.

Asanas   The Sanskrit term for the various postures of yoga.

Ayurveda   The science of life and longevity. 'Ayus' is the Sanskrit word for 'life' and 'veda' means 'science'.

Basti   One of the five methods of internal cleansing (panchakarma) used in Ayurveda. Either a medicated decoction or oil enema is used to cleanse the intestines of excess Vata dosha and as a method of systemic detoxification and rejuvenation.

Brahma murta   The hours of 3a.m. to 6a.m. which are said to be the 'time of knowledge' according to yogic and Ayurvedic wisdom. It is the point in time when our minds are most perceptive and receptive and is therefore considered the best time for acquiring knowledge.

Chakras   The seven energy centres of the body according to the teachings of yoga.

Churna   A medicated powder used as a medicine.

Doshas The biological humours (Vata, Pitta and Kapha) which govern all the psychobiological functions of the mind and body according to Ayurvedic wisdom.

Ghrita A medicated form of ghee (clarified butter).

Gunas The 20 qualities from which all animate and inanimate substances are composed, e.g. heavy, light, soft, hard.

Kapha One of the three doshas or biological humours. Kapha is composed of earth and water and is responsible for the physical structure of the body. The word Kapha means 'to stick'.

Kati basti A hands-on method of healing in which medicated oils or decoctions are applied to the lower back.

Kwath A decoction of medicinal substances.

Mandagni The state when the digestive fire is weakened or sluggish and thus unable to digest food properly. It leads to the build-up of ama, improper tissue nourishment and eventually disease.

Mantra The repetition of a sacred sound, meaningful word or phrase to promote a meditative state. The word means: 'that which saves the mind'.

Namaste The traditional Indian method of greeting in which the palms of the hand are pressed together in front of the chest. Literally translated, the word namaste means: 'I bow to the god within you'.

Nasya One of the five methods of internal cleansing (panchakarma) in which medicated oils or powders are administered via the nostrils.

Netra tarpana A hands-on method of healing in which medicated oil or milk is applied to the eye area.

Ojas A by-product of the seven tissues of the body and the body's innate immunity factor. Various medicinal substances and mental practices can be used to build ojas. Its depletion leads to illness and can result in death.

Panchakarma The five methods of detoxification or internal cleansing which are used to eliminate ama (undigested toxins) and excess levels of the doshas from the tissues of the body and GI tract. They are vamana (vomiting therapy), virechana (purgative therapy), basti (medicated oil or decoction enemas), nasya (administration of medicines via the nose) and raktamoksha (various forms of blood-letting).

Panchamahabhutas   The five elements or building blocks of life – air, ether, fire, earth and water. They form the basis of the three doshas, Vata (air and ether), Pitta (fire and a little water), Kapha (earth and water).

Pinda sweda   A topical method of healing in which a hot bolus of medicated herbs is applied to the body to alleviate pain and discomfort.

Pitta   One of the three doshas or biological humours. Pitta is composed of the fire element and a little water. It governs all the metabolic and biochemical functions of the body and mind such as our intellect and digestive processes. The word Pitta means 'to cook'.

Prakriti   A person's innate constitution or mind–body type, which is formed at the point of their conception and is unchanging throughout a person's life.

Pranayama   Controlled breathing techniques. One of the eight limbs of yogic philosophy.

Rajas   One of the two mind doshas. If Rajas is upset it has the power to cause mental health problems. Rajas is active, mobile and dynamic. When Rajas is aggravated it causes mental anguish and agitation.

Rajasic   An experience or substance which increases the quality of Rajas in the mind.

Raktamoksha   One of the five methods of internal cleansing (panchakarma), in which leeches or venesection are used as a method of blood-letting.

Rasa   The initial taste of a food as it is taken into the mouth and before it is digested. There are six tastes: sweet, sour, salty, bitter, pungent and astringent. Each has a specific effect on the doshas of the mind and body.

Rasayana   Rejuvenation therapy, one of the eight branches of Ayurvedic medicine, which is used to build immunity (ojas) and promote longevity.

Samagni   The state in which the digestive fire is functioning normally and at its optimum ability.

Samanya Vishesha   The law of similarity and dissimilarity which teaches us that like substances and experiences increase their like and opposites reduce their opposing qualities. A cold substance reduces heat, for example. This law forms the basis of the Ayurvedic approach to the promotion of good health and treatment of any disease.

Sattva   One of the three qualities of the mind. It is the state of supreme enlightenment, which delivers peace, clarity and purity of perception.

Sattvic   An experience or substance that builds the quality of Sattva in the mind.

Shirobasti   A hands-on method of healing in which a medicated oil or decoction is poured into a type of hat fitted to the top of the head.

Shirodhara   A hands-on method of healing in which a warm medicated oil or decoction is applied to the third eye (forehead) in a steady stream for a prolonged period.

Shiropichu   A hands-on method of healing in which a medicated oil or decoction is massaged into the head.

Shukra dhatu   The seventh tissue of the body, the reproductive tissue.

Tamas   One of the two doshas of the mind. It has the power to cause mental health problems such as depression. It is the quality of dullness, darkness and inertia. An excess of Tamas brings about ignorance, laziness and lethargy.

Tamasic   An experience or substance that increases the quality of Tamas in the mind.

Tiksnagni   The state when the digestive fire is overactive causing food to be burned up too quickly, so leading to poor nutrition and potentially to disease.

Udvartana   A form of dry massage in which rough, therapeutic powders are applied to the body in synchronized strokes.

Vamana   One of the five methods of internal cleansing (panchakarma). Vamana – a form of emesis or vomiting therapy – is generally used to treat Kapha-related problems such as asthma and as a method of detoxification.

Vata   One of the three doshas or biological humours. Vata is composed of air and ether. It is the subtle energy responsible for all our neurological functions and all movement in the body such as the processes of respiration and peristalsis. The word Vata means: 'to move, spread, flow'.

Vikriti   The state when an individual's original constitution is upset by one or more of the three doshas becoming imbalanced. An upset can lead to disease.

Vipaka   The post-digestive taste of any ingested food or medical substance, which has the power to influence the doshic balance of the mind and body.

Virechana   One of the five methods of internal cleansing (panchakarma). A purgative form of medication which is used to treat Pitta-related conditions and as a general method of detoxification.

Virya   The thermal potency of an ingested food or medicinal substance. It can be either hot or cold and has the power to influence the doshic balance.

Vishamagni   The state when the digestive fire is erratic, sometimes fast, sometimes slow. It is a form of improper digestion and has the power to cause disease.

index

acid indigestion **198**
acne **179–80**
agni (digestive fire) **93, 180**
air **11, 12, 13–14**
alcohol dependence **110**
alcohol intake **142, 145**
allergies **45, 176, 206**
ama
  eliminating **39, 40, 65–6, 185, 200–1**
  identifying **29–30**
Amalaki **168, 194**
anxiety **58, 181–2**
appetite, low **180**
Arjuna **168–9**
aromatherapy massage **38**
arthritis **182–3**
asafoetida **159–60**
Ashwagandha **169, 200**
asthma **184–5**
autumn/fall guidelines **143–4**
Avipathika churna **66, 175**

bad breath **185**
balding **185–6**
bedtime routine **139**
benefits of Ayurveda **4**
Bhastrika (breath of fire) **140, 150–1, 205**
biological humours see doshas
black pepper **160**

body clocks **25**
bowel habits **116**
brahmi **169**
breakfast **137–8**
breathing see prananyama (breathing techniques)
brittle nails **187**

cardamom **161**
cellulite **187**
chronic fatigue **188**
Chyawanaprash **175–6**
cinnamon **161–2**
cloves **162**
coffee **109**
colds **188–9**
constipation **36, 115, 116, 117, 189–90**
coriander **162–3**
coughs **190–1**
cumin **163**
cystitis **191**

daily routines **113–39**
  evening **139**
  morning **114–38**
dairy products **10, 106, 107**
  and mind–body type **94, 97, 99**
  properties of **85–6**
Dashamoola kwath **176**

depression 192–4
detoxification 31
　fasting 40–5
　seven-day diet 65–7
diabetes 34, 75, 194–5
diarrhoea 195
diet 6, 7, 8, 71–111
　alternatives to common
　　addictions 109–10
　balancing agni 93
　breakfast 137–8
　fasting 41–3, 196
　　post-fasting 43–5
　food combining 106
　food as a form of medicine
　　71–2
　food properties chart 76–92
　healthy eating habits 103–5
　and holistic healing
　　acid indigestion 198
　　acne 179
　　arthritis 182
　　asthma 184
　　bad breath 185
　　brittle nails 187
　　colds and flu 189
　　constipation 190
　　cystitis 191
　　depression 192, 193
　　diabetes 194
　　diarrhoea 195
　　fever 195
　　flatulence 196
　　heartburn 198
　　hypertension 199
　　jetlag 201
　　low appetite 180
　　obesity 204–5
　　osteoporosis 205–6
　key therapeutic foods in
　　Ayurveda 107–9
　meat eating 71–2
　and mind–body type 75–93
　　dual constitutional types 64,
　　　65, 101–2

　　Kapha types 63, 71, 98–101,
　　　102, 103, 223–7
　　Pitta types 62, 71, 96–8, 102,
　　　103, 186, 218–23
　　Vata types 60, 71, 93, 93–6,
　　　102, 103, 213–18
　pacifying disease 35–6
　rejuvenation therapy
　　(rasayanas) 46–7
　removing causes of disease 34
　seasonal guidelines 140–1,
　　141–2, 143, 144
　seasons and time of day/life
　　102–3
　and taste 72–5
　weight loss 101
digestion 29–31
　ama in the system 29–30, 39,
　　40, 65–6, 185, 200–1
　Ayurveda medicines 175, 176
　balancing agni 93
　and detoxification 31
　faulty 30–1
　rekindling digestive fire 35
　seven-day diet to cleanse and
　　fortify 65–7
dill 164
disease prevention 6, 26–7, 34–5
　and food as medicine 71–2
　see also healing; health
doshas 12–17, 18, 19
　and aromatherapy essences 38
　dosha-finding questionnaire
　　52–8
　and the law of similarity and
　　dissimilarity 22–3
　and life stages 23–4
　see also Kapha; Pitta; Vata
drinks 141, 143, 144
　early morning 115
　fasting 42–3
　lassi 142
　and mind–body type 96, 98,
　　100–1
dry skin 206

earth **11, 12, 15**
eggs, properties of **86**
the environment **27**
ether **11, 12, 13–14**
evening routine **139**
exercise **28, 206**
  and the ageing process **24**
  morning routine **117–35**
  seasonal guidelines **140, 141, 142, 145**
  see also yoga

fasting **40–5, 196**
fennel **164**
fenugreek **165**
fever **196**
fire **11, 12, 14**
fish
  and mind–body type **94, 97, 99**
  properties of **86–7**
five elements
    (panchamahabhutas) **10–12**
flatulence **196**
flu **188–9**
food see diet
fruit **106**
  and mind–body type **95, 98, 100**
  properties of **76–8**

garlic **165–6**
ghee **106, 107–8**
ginger **166**
gotu kola **170**
grains
  and mind–body type **94–5, 97, 99–100**
  properties of **83–4**
Guduchi **170, 194**
Guggulu **171, 204**
gunas (20 qualities) **18–19**

hangovers **197–8**
Haritaki **171–2, 194**

headaches **197**
healing **33–47**
  holistic methods of **179–209**
  pacifying disease **35–9**
  purging
    fasting **40–5**
    panchakarma **35, 39–40**
  rasayanas (rejuvenation therapy) **45–7**
  removing causes of disease **34–5**
health **22–32**
  definition of **4–5**
  and digestion **29–31**
  and internal body clocks **25**
  and the life cycle **23–4**
  and the mind **25–7**
  protecting immunity **31–2**
  and the seasons **24–5**
  and the senses **28–9**
  and wise living **27–9**
health problems **7, 18**
heartburn **198**
herbal remedies **45, 158–75**
  rasayanas **67–8**
herbal teas **110**
herbs, properties of **89–92**
hingvastaka churna **66, 176**
holistic methods of healing **179–209**
honey **11, 106, 108–9**
hygiene **6**
hypertension **198–9**

immunity protection **31–2**
Indian cultural practices **6**
insomnia **199–200**
irritable bowel syndrome (IBS) **58, 200–1**

jetlag **201**

Kapalabhati
    (cleansing breath) **150, 190**

Kapha
  daily routine for Kapha types
      114, 117, 136, 138, 139
  diet and Kapha types 63, 71,
      98–101, 102, 103, 223–7
  dosha 15, 16, 17, 18, 19
  and healing 38, 39
      fasting 41, 42, 44
      headaches 197
      menstrual problems 203
  and health 22, 23, 24, 25, 31–2
  healthy living tips 62–4
  herbal rejuvenation 68
  identifying mind–body type
      54–7
  imbalances 58
  Pitta-Kapha types 65, 101
  types of depression 192–3
  typical features of Kapha types
      62–3
  Vata-Kapha types 57, 65, 101
  yoga for Kapha types 132–5
kati basti 37
Kumari (aloe vera) 172

law of similarity and dissimilarity
    22–3
life stages 23–4
lunch-time routine 138–9

mantras 154–5
massage
  self-massage 38–9, 116–17,
      208
  therapeutic 37–8
meat
  and mind–body type 94, 97, 99
  properties of 86, 87
medicines
  authentic Ayurveda 175–7
  herbal 158–75
meditation 152–6, 200, 209
  on elements of nature 153–4
      empty bowl 152–3

mantras 154–5
  morning routine 137
  So-Hum 153
menopause 201–2
menstrual problems 202–3
mental rasayanas 68–9
mercury 11
Meshashringi 172, 194
migraine 203–4
milk 106, 107
mind and body 5, 8, 25–7
mind doshas 16–17
mind–body type (prakriti) 17–18,
    19
  and diet 93–102
  dual constitutional types 64–5,
      101–2
  identifying 52–8
  see also Kapha; Pitta; Vata
morning routines 114–38
mung-bean soup 41

neem 173
negative thoughts/emotions 26–7
nutmeg 166–7
Nutrigenomics 71
nuts
  and mind–body type 95–6, 98,
      100
  properties of 87–8

obesity 204–5
oils
  and mind–body type 96, 98
  properties of 89
oral vaccination 6
origins of Ayurveda 5–6
osteoporosis 205–6

pacifying disease 35–9
panchakarma (internal cleansing)
    35, 39–40, 140, 185, 186
panchamahabhutas (five
    elements) 10–12

pimples 207
pinda sweda 37
Pitta
    daily routine for Pitta types 114,
        117, 136, 138
    diet and Pitta types 62, 71,
        96–8, 102, 103, 186,
        218–23
    dosha 14, 15, 16, 17, 18, 19
    and healing 38, 39, 40
        depression 192
        fasting 41, 42, 44
        headaches 197
        menstrual problems 203
        migraine 203
    and health 22, 23, 24, 25
    healthy living tips 62
    herbal rejuvenation 68
    identifying mind–body type
        54–7
    imbalances 58, 175
    Pitta-Kapha types 65, 101
    seasonal routine 142
    typical features of Pitta types
        60–1
    Vata-Pitta types 64, 101
    yoga for Pitta types 129–32
plastic surgery 5
prakriti see mind–body type
        (prakriti)
prananyama (breathing
        techniques) 136, 147–51
    alternative nostril breathing
        143, 149, 188
    Bhastrika (breath of fire) 140,
        150–1, 205
    Kapalabhati (cleansing breath)
        150, 190
    Shitali (cooling breath) 149–50,
        198
    Ujjayi (breath of victory) 151,
        209
pregnant women 177
psoriasis 206

pulses
    and mind–body type 95, 97,
        100
    properties of 84–5
Punanarva 173–4, 203

Rajas 16
rasayanas (rejuvenation therapy)
        45–7, 67–9
    and diabetes 194
    herbal 67
    mental 68–9
rashes 206
rejuvenating elixir
        (chyawanaprash) 175–6
rejuvenation therapy (rasayanas)
        45–7, 67–9
rice 109

salt 109
Sanskrit 10
Sattva 16
seasons 140–5
    and diet 102–3
    influence on health 24
seeds
    and mind–body type 95–6, 98,
        100
    properties of 88–9
self-massage 38–9, 116–17
senses
    exercising 115–16
    using and abusing 28–9
seven-day detoxification diet
        65–7
Shatavari (wild asparagus) 174,
        202, 205–6
shirobasti (Indian head treatment)
        186
Shirodhara 5, 36–7, 199
Shitali (cooling breath) 149–50,
        198
Sitopaladi churna 176
skin problems 206–7

sleep **25, 139**
sore throat **207–8**
spices
　and mind–body type **96, 98,
　　100**
　properties of **89–92**
spring guidelines **140–1**
stomach ache **028**
stress **26, 38, 208–9**
sugar **110**
summer guidelines **141–3**
sweeteners
　and mind–body type **96, 98,
　　100**
　properties of **82–3**

Tamas **16**
taste **72–5**
therapeutic massage **37–8**
three doshas (biological humours)
　　see doshas
time of day/life
　and diet **102–3**
　influence on health **23–5**
tomatoes **110**
Trikatu **36, 41, 66, 176**
Triphala **36, 45, 177, 190, 194**
turmeric root **167**

Ujjayi (breath of victory) **151, 209**
urticaria **207**

Vata
　daily routine for Vata types **114,
　　117–18, 136, 138, 139**
　diet and Vata types **60, 71, 93,
　　93–6, 102, 103, 213–18**
　dosha **13–14, 15, 16, 17, 18**
　and healing **38, 39**
　　depression **192–3**
　　fasting **41, 42, 44**
　　headaches **197**
　　insomnia **199–200**
　　menstrual problems **202–3**

　　and health **22, 23, 24, 25, 31–2**
　　healthy living tips **60**
　　herbal rejuvenation **67**
　　identifying mind–body type
　　　54–7
　　imbalances **58**
　　typical features of Vata types
　　　58–60
　　yoga for Vata types **125–8**
Vata-Kapha types **57, 65, 101**
Vata-Pitta types **64, 101**
vegetables
　and mind–body type **95, 97–8,
　　100**
　properties of **78–82**

waking up time **114–15**
washing **117**
water **11, 12, 15**
weight loss **101, 177**
Western lifestyle **6–7**
wheat **106, 107, 109**
winter guidelines **144–5**
wise living **27–9**
work **138**
wrinkles **207**

yastimadhu **174–5**
yoga **118–35, 140**
　and holistic healing **194, 195,
　　206**
　Kapha types **132–5**
　Pitta types **129–32**
　sun salutation **119–25**
　Vata types **125–8**